Four Pillars to
Strengthen
Your Faith

Mark Verschueren

Four Pillars to
Strengthen
Your Faith

Learn What Faith Looks Like in Real Life

Love
God's Word
Speaking and Believing
Patience

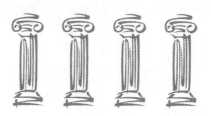

WestBow Press books may be ordered through booksellers or by contacting:

WestBow Press
A Division of Thomas Nelson
1663 Liberty Drive
Bloomington, IN 47403
www.westbowpress.com
1-(866) 928-1240

Because of the dynamic nature of the Internet, any web addresses or links contained in this book may have changed since publication and may no longer be valid. The views expressed in this work are solely those of the author and do not necessarily reflect the views of the publisher, and the publisher hereby disclaims any responsibility for them.

Certain stock imagery © Thinkstock.
Any people depicted in stock imagery provided by Thinkstock are models, and such images are being used for illustrative purposes only.

Scripture taken from the New King James Version. Copyright 1979, 1980, 1982 by Thomas Nelson, inc. Used by permission. All rights reserved.

Scripture quotations taken from the Holy Bible, New Living Translation, copyright 1996, 2004. Used by permission of Tyndale House Publishers, Inc., Wheaton, Illinois 60189. All rights reserved.

Scripture taken from the King James Version of the Bible.

Scripture taken from the New Century Version. Copyright © 2005 by Thomas Nelson, Inc. Used by permission. All rights reserved.

ISBN: 978-1-4497-7372-4 (e)
ISBN: 978-1-4497-7371-7 (sc)
ISBN: 978-1-4497-7370-0 (hc)

Library of Congress Control Number: 2012920769

Printed in the United States of America

WestBow Press rev. date: 11/15/2012

Contents

Pillar (pi-ler) – any upright supporting part

Revelation 3:12 - All who are victorious will become pillars in the Temple of my God, and they will never have to leave it. And I will write on them the name of my God, and they will be citizens in the city of my God—the new Jerusalem that comes down from heaven from my God. And I will also write on them my new name. NLT

Introduction

Faith. What is it, really? Is it something that we truly put stock or emphasis in, or is it just another word in the bible? In the 1990's, there were many charismatic churches and ministries that focused on "faith" teaching to the point that it almost became more of a symbol or even idol that people began to cling to rather than what God really intended it to be. It also began to breed almost a sense of entitlement or thought process that since I have "faith" in God then He owes me something. Again that is not God's character, nor does He owe us anything more than what He has already done for us through His Son Jesus Christ. So, is faith just a craze or a fad that people went through during this recent "faith movement?"

When I began writing this book, I had a friend of mine say to me that he felt the 'faith movement' to be a thing of the past and not what people need to hear anymore. I had to disagree with him strongly! In this time we live in, we need to have faith in God and what His Word says more than at any other time in history. I believe people are looking for leaders that will show them how to operate in faith. As leaders, we need to show them how much God desires to bless us through faith along with the authority we have as New Testament believers—which also takes faith. And this is not a faith that only exists to see what it can get from God but a faith that helps us love others, in spite of their (or our!) faults. A faith that helps us believe that God will bring us through the most dire of circumstances. And a faith that trusts God completely!

Faith has almost become flippant in its use. People say to others during times of trouble, "Have faith in God" or "Keep the faith," without giving it any substance. What I mean is this: if we are going to give comfort to someone who is struggling by saying something like, "Have faith in God," then we need to back it up with prayer and what God's Word says. Even before we do this, we need to wrap our arms around them in love. The simple words, "I am sorry for what you are experiencing", can do wonders for building a foundation to help them put their trust in God concerning what they are going through. We can't just throw "faith" around like it is just any other word, especially if we want to see it working in our lives.

Faith is more than just a word. It is an operating force in this world that can do great things for us, but only if we learn to use it and allow it to work for us. Faith is not just something that we automatically have, but as we study and meditate on it, we will see that it must become a way of life, a way of living.

My faith walk began over 17 years ago. Like any new Christian it began shakily. Although my heart was completely sold out to Christ it took time for me to begin to grow in my faith as I was challenged and encouraged by God's word and other strong Christian brothers and sisters. I have continued to grow through the years (I hope it never stops!) and while I have struggled at times with doubt during difficult times in my life

I have watched as God has orchestrated an amazing life for my family and I.

After working in a corporate setting for nearly 20 years I answered the call to full time ministry. After nearly six years of vocational ministry I can honestly day that our faith has been tested harder during this time than any other in our walk but God had also shown up and proved that when our hope is truly in Him we cannot fail!

Paul, in his teaching on the whole armor of God, gives us a great indicator of how we should be viewing faith as believers. Here is what it says in Ephesians chapter 6 (NKJ):

13 Therefore take up the whole armor of God, that you may be able to withstand in the evil day, and having done all, to stand.

14 Stand therefore, having girded your waist with truth, having put on the breastplate of righteousness, 15 and having shod your feet with the preparation of the gospel of peace; 16 above all, taking the shield of faith with which you will be able to quench all the fiery darts of the wicked one. 17 And take the helmet of salvation, and the sword of the Spirit, which is the word of God;

Notice what he says in verse 16: *"**Above all**, taking the shield of faith with which you will be able to quench all the fiery darts of the wicked one."* Out of all the pieces of armor that are given, faith is <u>above all</u>. Even above the sword of the Spirit which is the Word of God. Think about it. If we do not have faith, knowing that God's Word is the Truth, then the Bible is just a bunch of words. We must have faith in it and believe it. Only then will we be able to quench <u>all</u> the fiery darts of the wicked one.

Now, as long as we are talking about the armor of God, I need to help you see something that was brought to my own attention once. Notice that we are told to take up the whole armor of God. You really need to understand what this is saying. This is the armor of God! According to Genesis 1:26, we are created in God's image. So what does this mean? This is not just any armor that God wants us to use—which in itself would be enough—but this is the same armor that He Himself uses! It is the armor **of God!**

Something else I want you to get here is that God told us to put the armor of God *on*. Nowhere in the Bible does it tell us to take it off. Have faith in and believe God's Word! It will bring a whole new revelation of how we should be living our lives for Him.

As we go through this study on faith, I hope you will begin to see, just as I have, that faith truly is a driving force in our lives, one that must be lived out every day to have the freedom that God desires for us to have. It starts with our confession that Jesus is Lord and believing in our hearts that He was raised from the dead (Rom 10:9). Then, as you will see in this book, it goes way beyond that, if we desire it to.

Though our salvation is the most important step of faith that God desires for us to take, it is not where He wants us to stop. Jesus went to the cross to bring us victory in *every* part or our lives. Of course, we must understand that this power that comes from living a life of faith is not there for our own selfish use. This divine power, described in 2 Peter chapter 1, is there to help us live a godly life in order to build God's kingdom and glorify Him (verse 3). Living in this kind of faith brought to us by Jesus who is the author and finisher of our faith (Heb. 12:2), will launch us into the Great Commission that Jesus has given us. When people see us living a life with that God kind of faith, they will want it too and their hearts will be opened to receive the greatest gift of all, Jesus Christ as their Savior.

There are four main areas we are going to study and, I believe, are pillars in our walk of faith. These areas are God's Word (the Bible), Love, Speaking/Confessing and Believing, and Patience. I will cover these areas in their order of importance.

As we begin this study, please understand that this is not everything that it takes to see faith work in our lives.. While there are biblical references and verses that my wife Stephanie and I found to be very effective, it took allowing God to speak to our hearts in order for faith to become a lifestyle that we live.

Love

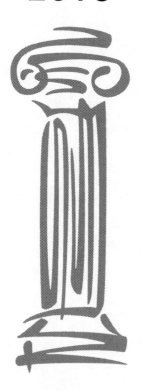

"Love is patient and kind. Love is not
jealous or boastful or proud ⁵ or rude.
It does not demand its own way. It is
not irritable, and it keeps no record
of being wronged. It does not rejoice
about injustice but rejoices whenever
the truth wins out. Love never gives up,
never loses faith, is always hopeful, and
endures through every circumstance."

- 1 Corinthians 13:4-7

Love Moves

While love may be the second Pillar in our study of what strengthens your faith, I believe it may be the most important. Jesus told us in Matt. 22:37 (NKJ) to *"Love the Lord your God with all your heart, with all your soul and with all your mind. This is the first and great commandment. And the second is like it. You shall love your neighbor as yourself. On these two commandments hang all the law and the prophet."*

Listen to what Jesus is saying! On these two commandments hang <u>all</u> the law. He is saying that if we are not walking in love, our faith is not going to move. When the revelation of how important this was to making my faith work hit me, my thinking changed radically. Paul backed this up in Gal. 5:6, saying that faith works by love.

God so desires for us to realize that He loves us. His love for us is extreme, and He wants our love for Him to be extreme. As that kind of love grows inside of us, it will begin to flow over and onto those around us, affecting every area of our lives too. I have people tell me I am an extremist in my faith for God. My response to them is, "Yes, I am extreme for God. I am extreme for God because He is extreme for me!"

In Ephesians 3:17-19 (NKJ), God's Word says, **"...that you, being rooted and grounded in love, may be able to comprehend with all the saints what is the width and length and depth and height – to know the love of Christ, which passes all knowledge; that you may be filled with all the fullness of God."**

Now that is extreme! Our Lord is telling us to get this idea so firmly grounded and planted into our hearts that we begin to live it without even thinking about it. If we become rooted and grounded in God's Word and His way of thinking, we will begin to comprehend His kind of love which is from everlasting to everlasting (Ps 103:17). And when we begin to live this way we will be filled with the fullness of God!

Ephesians 3:20 goes on to say, **"...*to Him who is able to do exceedingly abundantly above all that we ask or think....*"** God is love. 1 John chapter 4 teaches us that, but if we don't have that love inside of us, we will not believe that God wants and desires this kind of abundance for us. In fact, what it really says is that if we do not love or have this love inside of us, then we do not know God! When God's love is inside of us, it opens the door for our faith to work!

While studying the word 'love,' I found that, unlike the word 'faith' which is found primarily in the New Testament, 'love' is widely used throughout the entire Bible. In the Old Testament, God used the Hebrew words 'ahab' or 'ahabah.' The Hebrew translation for these words is literally "God's love towards man or His people." God shows us over and over in His Word that His love for us is unfailing and everlasting.

In Jer. 31:3 (NKJ), God spoke to Jeremiah saying, *"Yes, I have loved you with an everlasting love; therefore with loving-kindness I have drawn you."*

The word 'loving-kindness' in the verse above is the word 'chesed.' It means 'goodness, kindness, and faithfulness.' I take this to mean that His love is faithful and will not end just because I have not been perfect for Him. God is not looking for perfection but for hearts desiring Him!

In the New Testament, Jesus uses the word 'agape' or 'agapao' to teach us the same thing. These two words translated mean 'affection, love, benevolence and to be fond of or to love dearly.'

God shows us His love in so many ways and through so many different words. But it all boils down to this: God is telling us that His love is forever! He will never leave nor forsake us (Heb. 13:5). God loves us so much that He gave His one and only Son that we may be saved and have everlasting life (John 3:16).

The kind of love these words portray is not the kind of love we are used to seeing in our society today. It is not an emotional love. Our society has turned love into something touchy-feely. If we do not "feel it," then there must not be any love there. Consequently, we have a high divorce rates, even in the church family. Agape love stays, follows, and loves no matter what is happening or what the circumstances may be in a relationship.

Jesus taught this kind of love all throughout the New Testament. In Luke 6:27-31, Jesus teaches us to love our enemies. In verse 27, He says, ***"But I say to you who hear: Love your enemies, do good to those who hate you, bless those who curse you, and pray for those who spitefully use you."***

Wow! This seems impossible! How can we love and pray for men like those who took down the Twin Towers? Or closer to home, how can we pray for and bless those who speak unkindly to us in church or cut us off in traffic? Ouch, that one was for me! Or how do you respond lovingly to your wife who doesn't realize that you have had a hard day at work—thus, you think she does not care—and begins to unload on you all of her problems from the day? How can we possibly have that kind of love inside of us? This only comes by allowing God to put it there.

Romans 5:5 says, **"The love of God has been poured out in our hearts by the Holy Spirit who was given to us."**

God has given us, or put inside of us, the kind of Agape love that Jesus has commanded us to live by. It is up to us to push aside our flesh and live by it. My wife, Stephanie, knows this kind of love and has helped me to see and use it. Let me give you an example.

I have come home from a particularly long day at work and she began to update me about all *her* problems of the day. In a not so nice way, I proceed to tell her that if she would just do this or that, then she would not have those problems. Hurt and anger appeared in her eyes, and I could tell that an argument was about to break out—one I am, quite honestly, not ready for.

Remember, I had a long, hard day at work. At this point, as you can see, it was all about me.

But then that love that God had poured out into her heart took over. Her eyes softened and she looked at me and said, "Mark, I love you." Immediately, that love overflowed onto me, and I found myself filled with a love that covered all offenses and sin (1 Pet. 4:8). It did not matter what I had said or done. Stephanie made a choice to love me anyway, just like God does.

That is the kind of love that opens the door to faith. It is the kind of love that causes Paul to say that faith works by love. It is the kind of love that is in each Christian, if we **choose** to live by it. It is the kind of love that the devil cannot understand and has **no** defense against. Read it in God's Word. Meditate on it, and let it pour into your heart. Seek it and God will reward you with it (Heb. 11:6).

As with anything in our lives that we know needs to change, it starts first by making a *decision* or choosing to make that change. Reading God's Word daily, meditating on it, and allowing it to feed our spirit will begin to prompt those desires in our heart. In Ps. 37:4, the psalmist writes, **"Delight yourself in the Lord and He will give you the desires of your heart."**

Contrary to the way that some read this verse, it does not mean that God will give us everything we want. It means that as we delight ourselves in God, *He* will put desires in our hearts that are good for us and will comfort us and bless us. Sometimes this is not an easy thing. Sometimes God will put desires in our hearts that our flesh does not like.

Several years ago, as I began to really delight in God's Word and in the Lord Himself through various means, He began to speak to or put desires in my heart. One of those desires was to be a better husband and spiritual leader to my wife. He showed me that I was not walking in the law of love that Jesus commanded for my marriage. He brought me to verses like 1 Cor. 13:4-7 and Eph. 5:25-28. These verses showed very clearly how I needed to love Stephanie…and I was falling short of it.

Did it hurt to have these realizations brought to my attention? Of course it did. It hurt my pride most of all. I had been a believer for several years by this time, and it was hard to accept that I had been so far off base in this important area of my life for so long. Regardless of that, I made the *choice* to obey without compromise those things that God was telling my heart to do. Let me tell you, the results from sowing that good seed far outweighed the initial hurt I felt when God first placed that desire in my heart. I began to see a side of Stephanie that I never knew existed, and it was amazing to watch her blossom into the person that God really desired her to be. Our marriage went to a whole new level!

So, I am saying that it takes commitment to allow the law of love to work in our lives—a commitment to read God's Word daily, to allow it to speak to our hearts, and then to commit to making a *choice* to act on what He has shown us. This may sound like a difficult thing to do, but as you begin to make this commitment, you will begin to have a passion and excitement for God's Word that you never knew existed! It was always there, it just needed a little fanning to get the flame going.

The promises that come from walking and living in the law of love are numerous and exciting. There is so much that this simple little four letter word '*love*' will do for us in our lives. I am going to share some of these with you, but I want to encourage you to look these up in your own Bible. Go even further and look at other verses on love and see what they speak into your heart.

Faith Works by Love

In Galatians chapter 5, Paul tells us that faith works by love. In the Amplified Bible, it is translated this way: **"...but only faith activated and energized and expressed and working through love."**

So the Bible promises here that faith is activated or worked by love. As I shared in the first part of this study, allowing faith to operate in our lives is very important for us as Christians. The importance of it is made very clear by God in Hebrews 10:38 where God tells us, **"Now the just shall live by faith; But if anyone draws back, My soul has no pleasure in him."**

The first time I read this, I cringed. My heart cried out, "Oh Lord, please put this kind of faith inside of me!" But God spoke back to me saying, "There is nothing more I am going to do than what I did with My Son two thousand plus years ago. It has already been bought and paid for. You just need to grab a hold of it." Romans 12:3 tells us that God has given to each person *the* measure of faith. So, it was up to me again. I had to choose to walk it out. As I did this, it created a passion in me to share this faith with others.

Love Casts Out Fear

Another promise that is given to us by God with the word 'love' is in 1 John 4:18 (NKJ), which says, *"There is no fear in love; but perfect love cast out all fear, because fear involves torment."*

You must understand that fear is a spirit. It is a demonic spirit from the Devil who, if we allow him to, will make our lives a living hell. But we are assured in God's Word, in 2 Tim. 1:7 (KJ), that **"God hath not given us a spirit of fear, but of power and love and of a sound mind."**

If we are living and walking in the kind of love that Jesus commands us to, then there will not be room inside of us for fear to operate. Fear is the opposite of faith and is torment. Fear can debilitate us and keep faith from moving in our lives. If we have fear of sickness or diseases, then faith cannot work to keep us healthy. If we fear for our children's safety, then faith cannot work to keep the Devil from bringing destruction on them. If we fear for lack, then faith cannot work to bring us abundance. Fear will cause us to sin. It will cause us to steal, covet, lie and even murder. But perfect love will cast out all fear!

Look at what Paul shows us in Romans chapter 13:8-9 (NKJ): *"**Owe no one anything except to love one another, for he who loves another has fulfilled the law. For the commandments, 'You shall not commit adultery, You shall not murder, You shall not steal, You shall not bear false witness, You shall not covet,' and if there is any other commandment, are all summed up in this saying, namely, 'You shall love your neighbor as yourself.'"***

Fear is the basis of all of these sins because they are sins of the flesh. Our flesh fears to lose control over us. That fear comes into our consciousness, or our soul, and tries to govern our lives. If we allow the love that God has put inside of us to operate in our lives, then fear will be cast out. We must realize it is a constant battle against fear, or our flesh. It will try to drive out the love that our Father has deposited in our hearts!

As we fight this battle, our flesh will come into submission to our spirit, and we will begin to intensely desire to love our neighbors. As we begin to carry out this intense desire, we will find that there is no room for fear, and love will be the catalyst for every action we take. As this love begins to take action in our lives, faith will be activated because, as we have already learned in Galatians 5:6, *faith worketh by love.*

So I urge you; do not allow fear to have a place in your life. In fact, if we as Christians allow fear to operate in our lives, then we are asking Jesus to go the cross over and over again. Take the authority that Jesus bought for us at the cross and use it to permanently cast fear out of your life. Allow the love that God has poured out into your heart by the Holy Spirit (Rom 5:5) to take its place so you can live the life of freedom that God desires for you!

Love Covers Sin

G od also promises us in Proverbs 10:12 (NKJ), **"But love covers all sin."**

And again in 1 Peter 4:8 (NKJ), "**And above all things have fervent love for one another, for love will cover a multitude of sins.**"

God is telling us through Peter that if we have the love of Jesus in us, then it will not matter what someone does or says to us. Love will cover the sin or offense and keep us from reciprocating in an unkind way. After a while, the person that has offended us will begin to be drawn in by this love, and before long, they will begin to respond in love themselves. After all, God's Word promises in 1 Cor. 13:8 that love never fails. We truly are more than conquerors through Him who *loved* us (Rom. 8:37). God also promises that this love that we gain through Him will never stop or go away.

Romans 8:38-39 tells us that "**...neither death nor life, nor angels nor principalities nor powers, nor things present nor things to come, nor height nor depth, nor any other created thing, shall be able to separate us from the love of God which is in Christ Jesus our Lord.**"

That love, and its availability to us, is forever! I know you are asking, "How in the world do we live that way?" Let me tell you, it is not easy and never will be—at least not until Jesus comes back for us. Trust me, I screw up plenty. I still find myself blasting things out of my mouth to Stephanie, or Tristan, or Corbin, or other people around me.

But, I have found that with this love that God has poured out into my heart, I am able to immediately repent and ask forgiveness from God and the person involved. Whereas, in the life that I used to live, not walking in love, I would let what I said fester inside of me. I would begin to have feelings of guilt and then anger towards the person or persons involved. The way we can keep that love in our hearts day by day by day is to continually feed on God's Word *day by day*, precept upon precept, and line upon line (Is. 28:10 NKJ).

As Paul writes in Romans 10:8, **"The word is near you, in your mouth and in your heart (that is the word of faith which we preach)."**

Again, in Romans 10:17, we read, **"So then faith comes by hearing and hearing by the word of God."**

I urge you; get into God's Word. Read it, pray over it, and meditate on it daily, and the love that God pours into your heart will pour over and into others all around you.

Love is the greatest gift of all. Everything that we read and God teaches us in the Bible is a result of love. God created man out of love. He continually, over and over, showed mercy and grace (Hesed) to the Israelites because of love. He made the ultimate sacrifice of sending His Son to die for us out of His intense love and desire for a restored relationship with us. Father God is the Great Romancer!

In His Word, He is continually telling us to follow Him (Joshua 14:9), trust Him (Psalm 50:15), let Him (Psalm 55:22), and love Him (Matthew 22:37). God is love (1 John 4:16). He who abides in love abides in God and God in him.

Paul writes in 1 Cor. 13:1, **"Though I speak with the tongues of men and angels, but have not love, I have become sounding brass and clanging cymbal."**

In other words, without love, all that we do or say is nothing but a bunch of loud noise that means nothing! He goes on to say in the next couple of verses that even if we have all kinds of gifts or skills and strengths, but we do not have love, it does not mean a thing.

1 Cor. 13:4-8 says, **"Love suffers long and is kind; love does not envy; love does not parade itself, is not puffed up; does not behave rudely, does not seek its own, it not provoked, thinks no evil; does not rejoice in iniquity, but rejoices in the truth; bears all things, believes all things, hopes all things, endures all things. Love never fails."**

And again, we read in 1 Cor. 13:13, **"And now abide faith, hope, love, these three; but the greatest of these is love."**

Where love abounds so does mercy, grace, and every other thing that is fruitful abound. It takes love for absolutely every part of our life to operate in victory. It takes love for our faith to work, and it takes faith to love the way we are commanded to.

God's
Word

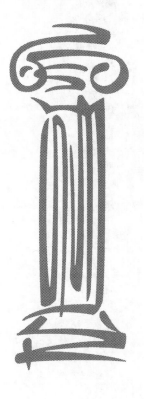

"All Scripture is given by inspiration of God, and is profitable for doctrine, for reproof, for correction, for instruction in righteousness, that the man of God may be complete, thoroughly equipped for every good work."

- 1 Timothy 3:16-17

It's Life Changing

Many years ago, like so many other new and very young Christians, I was on fire and very zealous for God and His Word. At that time, I knew that God was calling me into His ministry, and I threw myself into serving God and serving others—or at least I thought I was.

What I didn't realize was that as a newly zealous servant of our God I had a lot of past hurts, generational iniquities, and just general broken heartedness that needed to be dealt with before I could really move forward in my service for Him. You see, I was not a teen when I finally began to let God have complete control of my life. I wasn't even in my twenties. I was thirty-two years old when I really, truly gave the controls over to God.

What a change there was in my life! I began to see things in a whole new light, or really, I began to see things in **the Light** instead of in the darkness that I had been walking in almost my whole life. So, as I said, I tried to find as many things as I could to get involved with through our church.

Although these are all good things, sadly, I was doing them largely because I thought I needed to earn God's approval and the approval of those around me. It was what I knew—acting out, showboating and desperately seeking others' approval and acceptation. I had no idea about the Agape kind of love that Jesus teaches us in the Bible, the kind of love that accepts another nonjudgmentally and unconditionally regardless of the circumstances. I did not understand the verses in Ephesians 2:8-9 (NKJ) that tell us:

"For it is by grace you have been saved through faith, and that not of yourselves; it is the gift of God, not of works, lest anyone should boast."

I was young and immature as a Christian and got caught up in what many Christians think they must do and that is working, working, and working to win the approval of God.

I had been married to my beautiful wife Stephanie for nine years at the time this was all taking place. Our first baby, Tristan, was one year old and Stephanie was pregnant with our second. I was spending nearly every night out of the house doing what I felt was God's work and calling. This went on for about a year.

One night after Corbin had just been born, I was headed out the door to help with an inner city children's ministry I had become involved with. Stephanie stopped me at the door and with tears and pleading eyes said, "Mark, we need you at home. I need you at home." I actually got angry at her, said something really intelligent (yes, that is sarcasm!) about doing God's work, and stomped out the door.

I have to admit, my head was reeling as I drove to town that night. I spoke to God and asked Him if I was doing something wrong, and for the first time in my life I heard God speak to my heart. What He said was hard for me to accept, a truth I discovered that would often be repeated in my life as God dealt with me concerning various issues. This is what He said to my heart, *"Mark, your first ministry, after seeking Me, is your family. If you cannot be the spiritual leader in your home that I need for you to be, then I will never be able to use you in any ministry outside of the home."*

That one statement changed my life. I realized that I was not ready to be of use in other ministries and that there were some things in my life that needed to change. I began to focus my attention on seeking God through His Word and other people's teaching of the Word through books and tapes. Slowly, God began to mold, shape, and prepare me for the plans that He had for my life. God tells us in Jeremiah 29:11 (AMP):

"For I know the thoughts and plans that I have for you, says the Lord, thoughts and plans for welfare and peace and not for evil, to give you hope in your final outcome."

You see, God already knew exactly what His plans and desires for us were before we were ever born (Jeremiah 1:5), but those plans and desires will never come to pass if we are not seeking, desiring and making Jesus Lord of every part of our lives.

Now I want to share something with you that I feel like God is asking me to share. I think this will encourage some of you who are going through the same awesome transformation of spirit, soul and body that I went through and continue to go through. This sudden change in my life, lifestyle, and overall attitude was difficult for Stephanie to accept. Let me explain why.

The first eight years of our marriage were very painful for Stephanie. I was a very angry, verbally abusive, and selfish man. To top all that off, I was an alcoholic. On my list of priorities my wife was very near the bottom. I thank God often that He gave her the grace to stay with me. So even though she saw God making this radical transformation in my life, she found it a little hard to believe. It took nearly two years of watching me persistently and consistently seeking God while treating her with the love and respect she deserved before she was ready to believe this was for real. Even more importantly she was able to forgive me all the wrongs I had done to her all those years. It was a huge step in our marriage relationship and in our walk with God. From this point on, she began to blossom into a beautiful, godly woman as I lovingly encouraged her to earnestly seek God for herself. Now she is sought after by many other women for her godly wisdom and advice.

Now you may be wondering how all this is relevant to the topic at hand. I wanted you to see where I had come from and the change God, through His Word, has made in me. You see, as I sought after God through His Word and prayer every day, my faith began to grow. My love for God and those around me grew also. I began to have faith that God could repair my marriage, bring health to my body, and prosperity to every area of my life. It was God's Word more than anything that brought about this ability to effectively use the faith God put inside of me. This alone has been more powerful than any wisdom given from a godly mentor or teaching from a pastor or lessons learned from any book or audio teaching. Although these are all important and necessary, it has been the constant and earnest seeking of God and His Word that has built my faith and made me into the man that God needed me to be.

Romans 10:17 says, "*So then, faith comes by hearing, and hearing by the word of God.*" God makes it very clear here that it is through His Word that our faith is built.

Matthew 6:33 says, "*But seek first the kingdom of God and His righteousness and all these things shall be added to you.*"

I mentioned before—and will again many times—that we must make God *first* in every part of our lives. Jesus must be Lord of **all**. It is the daily seeking of God through His Word, prayer, fellowship with other spirit filled believers, and teaching from a Word inspired church that will get your faith working for you. Now, notice what I said here. It gets your faith *working*, not *increase* it. You have all the faith that you need inside of you, and you are not going to get any more because God has given us all the same measure of faith (Rom. 12:3).

So now you may be thinking, "So how am I going to get this healing that I need or this breakthrough in my finances if God does not help me increase my faith?" Someone once said to me, "I need to get a faith like that." I had just shared with her about how our car had been given a terminal prognosis—the motor was having big problems—and we were either going to have to put a lot of money into it or just retire it. We had just been blessed with a large sum of money but knew that God had other plans for that money than dumping it into fixing a car. We saw the problem for what it really was. The Devil was trying to steal this seed before it could be sent out.

So this is what we did—though it may sound silly to some of you, but this is how strongly we believed in God's Word. We laid hands on that car and thanked God for mending any broken parts in it and then took authority over the situation and commanded that every part in that car work perfectly. Three days after we did this, that car began to run perfectly! I continued to drive it for a while, and then God asked us to sell it to sow the money into another ministry. I shared this with that person who, while praising God with me, wished she could get that kind of faith. I told her the same thing I am going to share with you right now. You already have it!

Look at Romans 12:3. It says, *"...as God has dealt to each one the measure of faith."*

When we accepted Jesus into our hearts and made Him Lord of our lives, we each were given the same measure of faith. We can't look at each other and say, "Well, I have more faith than so and so, or I wish I had as much faith as so and so." None of us has more faith than any other believer. We each have been given the **same** amount of faith. It is our belief or lack of belief that will send our mountain away or allow it to stay.

Let me show you something. Let's go to Matthew chapter 17, starting with the fourteenth verse. A very distraught man has just brought his son to Jesus, telling Him that his son is an epileptic and suffers severely. In actuality, the man's son was being controlled by a demonic spirit who was trying to kill the boy by throwing him into constant danger. Now look closely at the 16th verse (NKJ). It says, *"So I brought him to Your disciples, but they could not cure him."*

Let's stop right here for a moment. Why couldn't the disciples heal the boy? Was it their lack of faith? It couldn't have been, for two reasons. One, as Romans 12:3 declares, God has given each one of us the *same* measure of faith. And two, when this story took place, it was only a short time after Jesus had sent the twelve out and they "*...cast out many demons and anointed with oil many who were sick, and healed them" (Mark 6:13, NKJ).*

After seeing all the great things that were done through them using the name of Jesus, I seriously doubt their faith was weak when trying to heal the boy. So what was it? It was two things. It was the father's lack of faith **and** the disciples' lack of belief. They had unbelief in their hearts. Look at how Jesus addressed this in Matthew 17 again.

Look first at verse 17. It says, **"Then Jesus answered and said, 'O faithless and perverse generation, how long shall I be with you? How long shall I bear with you? Bring him here to Me.' And Jesus rebuked the demon and it came out of him, and the child was cured from that very hour."**

In other words, Jesus said, "Listen people, I am not going to be here forever so you need to get this! You need to realize My name, have faith in My name, and **believe** in the power of My name. Now look at verse 19-21 (NKJ) to see what Jesus said to the disciples.

He said, *"Then the disciples came to Jesus privately and said, 'Why could we not cast it out?' So Jesus said to them, 'Because of your unbelief; for assuredly, I say to you, if you have faith as a mustard seed, you will say to this mountain, 'Move from here to there,' and it will move; and nothing will be impossible to you. However this kind does not go out except by prayer and fasting.'"*

Now Jesus is showing us here that it is not a lack of faith that is the problem. He says that if we only have the faith of a mustard seed, a seed so small that if you hold it between your thumb and forefinger you can hardly see it, that anything is possible to us. However, if we have any amount of unbelief in us, it will hinder or completely stop the flow of faith.

This teaching on believing is not taught enough in the church today. The reason may be because many teachers and pastors are afraid they will push people away with this sort of teaching. They fear people will feel condemned because they don't have enough belief inside of them. But people need to hear this. And if it is presented as God's Word and done so in love, then people will accept it and begin to realize the power that resides within them. Jesus knew the importance of teaching this in the New Testament and did so without compromise. Throughout the New Testament, Jesus commands many that He spoke to, healed and delivered to believe and receive. He knew that unbelief was the single biggest hindrance to any of them receiving what they needed. Even as He prepared to leave the disciples, He spoke against their unbelief.

Look in Mark 16:14-18 (NKJ) where it is written, **"...and he rebuked their <u>unbelief</u> and hardness of heart, because they did not <u>believe</u> those who had seen Him after He had risen. And He said to them, "Go into all the world and preach the gospel to every creature. He who <u>believes</u> and is baptized will be saved; but he who does not <u>believe</u> will be condemned. And these signs will follow those who <u>believe</u>: In My name they will cast out demons; they will speak with new tongues; they will take up serpents; and if they drink anything deadly,**

it will by no means hurt them; they will lay hands on the sick, and they will recover."

Look at the number of times the word 'believe' or 'unbelief' are in this single passage of scripture! Jesus knew that belief had to dominate their thinking and have a permanent place in their hearts. Look again at verse 14 when He appeared to the eleven and rebuked their unbelief and hardness of heart. Jesus knew that the spirit of unbelief had to be cast out before the disciples could go out and do the work He had set before them. That spirit of unbelief is still prevalent today, trying to get into our heads and then into our hearts or our spirits. So how do we get rid of it? How do we fight this unbelief when sickness or disease threatens to debilitate us or our family is threatening to fall apart? By God's Word and seeking Him diligently.

For as Paul says in Hebrews 11:6 (NKJ), "...*for he who comes to God must believe that He is, and that He is a rewarder of those who diligently seek Him.*"

It takes knowing God through prayer and His Word to begin to build that belief up inside of us. If we do this and still struggle with unbelief, then we may need to spend some time in fasting and prayer.

Look with me again at Matt 17:21 (NKJ) where Jesus says, **"However this kind does not go out except by prayer and fasting."**

Jesus was not talking about the evil spirit in the boy, but of the spirit of unbelief that resided in their hearts. Jesus knew that it sometimes takes fasting to bring our flesh into submission. It is our five senses of seeing, feeling, hearing, tasting and smelling that threaten to overcome our belief of what Jesus has already done for us. In other words, our flesh will always battle against what has already been done for us. Faith is knowing the victory we have in every area of our lives, regardless of what our senses are trying to tell us. Fasting will bring our flesh into submission and allow our spirit to control our way of thinking.

Fasting also brings us into a closer communication with God. As we fast and pray and read God's Word, our spirit is strengthened and begins to dominate the soul or the thought life. But ultimately it is God and His word that takes us to that desired place. It will get rid of unbelief and it will strengthen our faith. It will take us to a place of believing or trusting in God's Word and the promises it gives us regardless of what is happening around us. Look at what Paul teaches us in Hebrews 11:1 (NKJ):

"Now faith is the substance of things hoped for, the evidence of things not seen."

It does not matter if we see the desired results or not, but we must believe and trust that God, in all His goodness, has already given us what we need in every situation. Psalm 34:8 (NKJ) says, **"Oh, taste and see that the Lord is good; blessed is the man who trusts in Him!"**

We have to trust in God and believe His Word to have the blessing. But just like with any relationship, it takes time to build trust, and we have to get to *know* God and His Word to build that kind of trust and in what He desires for us. As we fill our hearts with God's Word, it will become so full that when bad things come against us—and trust me, they will—we will have what we need inside of us to beat it. Romans 10:8 (NKJ) says, *"The word is near you, in your mouth and in your heart."* And also verse 10 says, *"For with the heart one believes unto righteousness, and with the mouth confession is made unto salvation."*

The word 'salvation' both here and all throughout the New Testament does not only mean the saving of our souls to spend eternity in Heaven with our Lord as so many Christians think. That is awesome in itself, but God wants us to realize more than that. If you look up the word 'salvation' in the Greek, we are given the idea of being rescued and brought to safety, having deliverance from oppression, and having health. So, it is very important to know what we are putting in our hearts. If we are filling it with all the junk that the world has to offer and not the power of God's Word, then we will not have what is needed to persevere in tribulation or persecution that is coming against us. The power of God's Word inside of us is truly awesome!,

"For the word of God is living and powerful, and sharper than any two edged sword, piercing even to the division of soul and spirit, and of joints and marrow, and is a discerner of the thoughts and intents of the heart" (Hebrews 4:12, NKJ).

So once again, the more we have God's Word inside of us, the more it resides in our hearts and thus overflows into every area of our lives, allowing our faith to work for us. Have the God kind of faith! As Jesus says in Mark 11:22, *"Have the faith of God."* There truly is power in God's Word if we allow ourselves to believe it and let our minds—or soul—be enlightened to the power already inside of us waiting to be used.

Paul, in his letter to the Ephesians, tried to get this point across in the first chapter. That letter was not just to the Ephesians, but to all believers in any era. Ephesians 1:1 reads, **"Paul, an apostle of Jesus Christ by the will of God, to the saints which are at Ephesus and to the faithful in Christ Jesus."**

If you are a believer, then you are the faithful in Christ Jesus! Now I want us to look at verses 16 through 23 (NKJ):

"Therefore I also, after I heard of your faith in the Lord Jesus and your love for all the saints, do not cease to give thanks for you in my prayers; that the God of our Lord Jesus Christ, the father of glory, may give to you the spirit of wisdom and revelation in the knowledge of Him, the eyes of your understanding being enlightened, that you may know what is the hope of His calling…"

I want to stop right here for a moment. Look at what Paul, by inspiration of the Holy Spirit, is saying. He prays first that God may give us wisdom and revelation in the knowledge of Him, or Jesus Christ. Paul prays that the eyes of our understanding are enlightened or open to the hope of His calling. In other words, he wants our minds (souls) to begin to understand what our spirit already knows. Our spirit already knows what the call and the will of God is for us, but our mind and our flesh have to be convinced.

Speaking of God's will, I want to go back to verse 9. People, the church, and religious tradition have tried to make God's will such a mystery, but Paul and God's Word speak to the contrary. Actually, it is the Devil who has tried to cloud our minds with religious tradition in an attempt to keep us from knowing the true grace of God. In verse 9 (NKJ), it reads, **"...having made known to us the mystery of His will, according to His good pleasure which He purposed in Himself."**

People have been taught by the church for ages that the will of God is this big mystery, and we just can't begin to know what His will is. That is not true. God uses His Word to reveal those mysteries. Just as Paul tried to teach us here in Ephesians, your spirit knows what the will of God is and desires for that revelation knowledge to be conveyed to the rest of you. However, this is only going to come by consistently feeding and edifying your spirit with God's Word. Now let's go back to Ephesians 1 (NKJ) to where we left off at verse 19:

"...and what is the exceeding greatness of His power toward us who believe, according to the working of His mighty power which He worked in Christ when He raised Him from the dead and seated Him at the right hand in the heavenly places, far above all principality and might and dominion, and every name that is named, not only in this age but also in that which is to come."

Now look with me at verse 19 where it says, "...what is the exceeding greatness of His power." The Word conveys the message that this is something that is already done. It then goes on to say that this greatness of His power is toward—or in—us who believe. I really want to help you understand what is being said here. God wants us to understand that the same great power that He used to raise Jesus Christ from the dead is inside each of us if we believe! Look at this same verse in the Amplified Bible:

"And (so that you can know and understand) what is the immeasurable and unlimited and surpassing greatness of His power in and for us who believe."

What an awesome Word! There is nothing that the Devil or life can try to bring against us that we cannot defeat with that power. God loves us so much that He not only sent His Son to die for us, but He raised Him up in victory and then gave us the same power that He used to raise Him up! But, we have to <u>believe </u>so that we have *faith*! God's Word says in Romans 10:17 (NKJ), *"So then faith comes by hearing, and hearing by the word of God."*

It takes that consistent and persistent pressing in on the Word of God to strengthen our faith and our belief in what God's Word tells us. We may read something in the Bible a hundred times, but then suddenly, one day, our soul and our flesh come to the realization of what our spirit already knew. This happens to me all the time. Just the other day, a passage I was reading in Romans finally sank in. I got so excited that I had to call Stephanie over to read it with me! I was reading in Romans Chapter 8 starting at verse 2. From the Amplified Bible:

"For the law of the Spirit of life (which is) in Christ Jesus (the law of our new being) has freed me from the law of sin and death."

God spoke to me that day, saying that He does not see me as a sinner. In my heart, I heard Him say, "I do not see you that way."

Now do not misinterpret what I am saying here. I am not saying that I do not sin—of course I sin. But when I do, I immediately submit myself before God and whoever or whatever I sinned against and repent. I am trying to say that we don't have to go around with our heads hung low and our faces so solemn, saying we are just a sinner who is too lowly and undeserving to receive any of God's blessings. That is just another lie from the Devil! He knows that if he can keep you feeling that way, then you will not be of any good to God and His kingdom. We **are not** just a lowly sinner, believing such is disrespecting God and what His Word tells us. Look with me at Ephesians chapter 2 verse 10 (NKJ):

"For we are His workmanship, created in Christ Jesus for good works, which God prepared beforehand that we should walk in them."

How do you think it makes God feel as we go around badmouthing ourselves when He showed us in His Word how awesome He thinks we are? We are His workmanship created for good works! God sees us as His masterpiece! God sees us according to His Spirit that is alive in us after we receive Jesus as our Lord and Savior.

God's Word is Alive and Powerful

G od's Word truly is alive and powerful! As we saw earlier in Hebrews chapter 4 verse 12 (AMP), it is written:

"For the word of God is alive and full of power(making it active, operative, energized, and effective); it is sharper that any two edged sword, penetrating to the dividing line of the breath of life(soul) and (the immortal)spirit, and of joints and marrow(of the deepest parts of our nature), exposing and sifting and analyzing and judging the very thoughts and purposes of the heart."

In other words, God's Word will circumcise our hearts. As we read it and allow the power of it to work on our lives, His spoken Word begins to reveal the sin that we need to repent of, or generational curses or iniquities that we need to cast out, or hardness of heart due to unbelief that we need to change and let go of. God speaks of this kind of circumcision all through the Old Testament. In Genesis 17:10 and 11 (KJ) God establishes this as a covenant of blood between Himself and man:

"This is my covenant, which ye shall keep, between Me and you and thy seed after thee; Every man child among you shall be circumcised. And ye shall circumcise the flesh of your

foreskin; and it shall be a token of the covenant betwixt Me and you."

God began very early on to use circumcision to establish a covenant with Himself by way of cutting away part of ourselves. He takes this to the heart in Deut. 30:6 (KJ):

"And the Lord thy God will circumcise thine heart and the heart of thy seed, to love the Lord thy God with all thine heart (your spirit) and with all thy soul that thou mayest live."

So going back to Hebrews chapter 4, God's Word is **alive** and **powerful** when we apply it to our lives. It first begins by letting God's Word *circumcise* all the junk out of our lives that is going to hinder that power. As this happens—and believe me, this is a lifetime process—God gives us understanding of the power of His Word. We then can take His Word and apply it to every area of our lives.

I can tell you from my own experience that it is awesome what the power of God's Word can and will do in your life. Look with me again at the last part of Deuteronomy 30:6 where God says, *"…that thou mayest live."* God doesn't just mean getting by in this life. No, He means for us to *live!* Take time to read through the blessing that He desires for us have in Deuteronomy 28 and begin to fully comprehend all that God wants for us. And don't let anyone tell you that the promises of the Old Testament blessings don't apply to us anymore. Galatians 3:29 (KJ) says, **"And if ye be Christ's, then are ye Abraham's seed and heirs according to the promise."**

Those same promises that God gave to Abraham and the people of Israel are for us as born again believers also! Jesus says in John 10:10 (KJ), **"The thief cometh not, but for to steal, and to kill, and to destroy; I am come that they might have life, and have it more abundantly."**

Jesus makes it very clear that He desires for us to have abundance in our life. This doesn't apply to only a few areas of our lives, but it covers <u>every</u> area of our lives! He wants us to have abundance in our health, in our relationships, in our finances, and especially in our relationship with Him! Get God's Word inside of you! I am going to say that from time to time. Read it, meditate on it, pray on it, listen to teaching on it, and let His power dominate your life.

Seek God First!

J esus teaches us to seek, or go to, God first for all of our needs. He is trying to show us that if we will make God first in every part of our lives, then <u>all</u> of our needs will be met. Look with me again at Matthew 6:33. I especially like the translation from the Amplified bible:

"But seek (aim at and strive after) **first of all His kingdom and His righteousness** (His way of doing and being right), **and then all these things taken together will be given to you besides."**

This verse was a foundational verse for me in my early Christian walk. When I first read this verse, I was awestruck by the simplicity of it. I thought, "If I just seek God, I can stop **worrying** about how am I going to pay those bills or how am I going to keep my marriage intact or any other concern I have in my life?" Yes! Jesus is asking us to stop looking to ourselves or others for the answer and look to God and His Word.

God spoke to me strongly concerning this (not looking to ourselves and others for answers first) when I first went into the ministry full time. I had just been asked to come on full time as an associate pastor, and I was having all these thoughts in my head—wonder who put them there—about whether I was capable of doing the job. I especially struggled with these thoughts for the first couple of days when, one day, I was praying about it and God spoke to me. Basically He said, "Would you shut up! Get your eyes and thoughts off yourself and get them on Me. By yourself! You cannot accomplish anything, but with Me, all things are possible (Matt. 19:26). Let Me lead and you will be just fine." Then He brought to remembrance Matt. 6:33. Of course, I repented immediately and God brought peace back into my life.

When I was a table leader in a men's ministry at our church, I brought this verse into nearly every meeting that I taught and ministered at. I used to say to them, "I know you hear me say this all the time, but I really want you to understand the importance of it. I promise you, if you will live your life by this verse and put God first in every area, all the issues you are telling me about will be taken care of."

Yes, there will be battles, but we need to go into these battles having already put God first and believing we will win because of what God has done for us. I believe Jesus uses this simple verse to get us to seek after God more, knowing that as we do this, our faith in God and His Word would begin to grow. Only then will the force and power of that faith begin to move in our lives.

I shared with you earlier in this book how God radically changed my life, so I know personally how powerful this force is. Let me share with you another example. I had the privilege of seeing this transformation happen to a gentleman who started sitting at my table at church. He came to our table as a young

Christian, just recently born again. He was older than I and very quiet, but he showed up consistently week after week. After a period of time, he began to share with us where his life was at. It was a sad but familiar story. He had spent his life pursuing only his own interests through work and other activities, and consequently, he had pushed his family completely away from him. I remember seeing the deep sense of sorrow and remorse in his eyes, and my heart really went out to him because I knew what he was feeling. I kept taking him back to Matthew 6:33 and told him over and over to make this verse the foundation of his life.

Well, I began to see God's Word become alive to him, finding a hold in his heart and life. He began to talk more at the table, and I saw a light in his eyes that had not been there before. His faith began to grow and became a force in his life. He went to his children and apologized, asking for their forgiveness. Of course, it was a little hard for them to accept, considering the kind of person he had been before, but he did not lose heart.

I was called away from that ministry and did not get an opportunity to witness all that God continued to do in this man's life, but about a year later, I had a chance to talk to the person that took over the table I once lead. That man not only had reconciled with his family, but more importantly, his faith in and desire for God was leading his life. What an awesome testimony! This man *chose* to believe and have faith in what God's Word promises.

We all have that choice. We can choose to put God first in every area of our lives and thus have blessings in every area. Or we can hold back, remain un-submitted to God, and have curses in every area. God gives us the same choice that He gave the people of Israel in Deuteronomy 11:26-28: blessings or curses. Which will you choose? I choose blessings! I choose to live with the victory that Jesus so willingly and dearly paid for, even when I was a sinner (Romans 5:8)! I choose to live by the words that Joshua so boldly pronounced to his fellow Israelites in Joshua 24 verse 14, *"Serve the Lord!"* And again, in verse 15, he said, *"But as for me and my house, we will serve the Lord!"*

It takes **faith** to live this way. It takes a boldness that will seem overly extreme or strange to some people. But mostly, it takes faith to live completely committed and submitted to God's Word, to live it without compromise in every area of our life. In essence, it means to live as Jesus commands us in Matthew 6:33. So seek first the Kingdom of God and His righteousness and all these things *shall be added to you!*

Does It Really Work?

Now, I want to talk to you and prepare you for what is almost certainly going to happen when you make the choice to live completely and wholeheartedly for God and His Word. The Devil will come immediately to try and steal the Word that has been planted into our hearts (Mark 4:15). How does this happen? Let me give you an example in my own life.

Our church had begun a building campaign and Stephanie and I had been praying about what we should sow. We prayed and sought God and prayed some more. Finally, the morning to turn in our pledge card came, and I was praying alone in our reading room when God gave me a vision of a dollar amount on a chalkboard. I went and found Stephanie, who was in another room in the house praying about the same thing, and asked her if God had given her anything. She had and gave me the exact figure that God had showed me in the vision! Now we were excited, because we knew this was from God but we were also intimidated because it was way, way more than we had ever given before. I sat down and put it on paper along with the other things that were in our budget. On paper, I could not see how we were going to do it, but we knew that we needed to trust in God. So we put God first in this situation, standing on His Word, particularly in 2 Corinthians 9:8-10:

"And God is able to make all grace abound toward you, that you, always having all sufficiency in all things, may have an abundance for every good work...Now may He who supplies seed to the sower, and bread for food, supply and multiply the seed you have sown and increase the fruits of your righteousness while you are enriched in everything for all liberality, which causes thanksgiving through us to God."

We were standing on this Word, knowing that God would supply. Here is where the enemy comes in to steal the Word from your heart. Almost immediately, we had attacks on our finances with two large and unexpected repair bills, one on our house and one on a car. Of course, the Devil began putting thoughts in our heads, telling us that we could not afford the commitment we had made and that we needed to be more realistic in our commitment. For about a week, I struggled with doubt and unbelief and finally just had to tell the Devil to shut up! Stephanie and I came back together in prayer and remembered the vision that God had given us and the promise found in 2 Corinthians. We then took our authority and told the Devil to get his hands off our finances, in Jesus' name. Things did not change immediately, we had to be patient and let out faith work. We stood strong on God's Word, seeking him diligently and He rewarded us just as He promised (Heb. 11:6). We were blessed in such a way through my job that not only were we able to fulfill our commitment to the building campaign, but we were also able to bless others in various ways that God asked us to.

In John 10:10, Jesus says that the thief does not come except to steal, to kill, and to destroy. And again, in John 16:33, He says that in this world we will have tribulation, but He follows both of these statements with words of victory. In John 10:10, Jesus says that He come that others might have life and that they may have it more abundantly. In John 16:33, He ends the verse with this statement, "...*but be of good cheer, I have overcome the world.*"

I promise you, just as Jesus told us, the enemy will attack. The life of a Christian is not for the weak hearted. When I say 'Christian,' I don't mean the person who attends church once a week to make themselves feel good and to impress others. Neither am I talking about the person who may have a good knowledge of God's Word but uses it as a sword to cut other people instead of using it against the enemy like it is supposed to be. The Christian I am talking about is the person who is passionate for God's Word and is ready to be a warrior in a fight that will not end until Jesus comes back for us all. They are the ones who take God's Word and wield it as a weapon to protect not only themselves, but those around them.

God, as our Supreme Commander, expects us to be the kind of warrior that is willing to speak and act as Paul did. We should rather be willing lose our salvation and spend eternity in Hell than see one person around us reject Jesus as their Savior. The life of a true Christian is not easy. In fact, as you grow and mature in your walk with God, you will find that intense attacks will come.

I remember when we first made the decision to answer God's call to go into the ministry full time. For about 1 or 2 months, we were attacked from every side. Our health was attacked, and as soon as we cast out the sickness, our finances were attacked, and as soon as we rebuked that, the Devil attacked our thoughts by telling us we were making the wrong decision and going in a direction we were not supposed to go. But, we remembered what Jesus said, "I have overcome the world! I come that you may have life and have it more abundantly!"

It takes **faith** and courage to be able to live this way. It takes the ability to **believe** without compromise in what God's Word promises us. We must **believe** in our **hearts** that we have the authority God gave us. Jesus says in Luke 10:19 (NKJ), **"I give you the authority to trample on serpents and scorpions and over all the power of the enemy, and nothing shall by any means hurt you."**

Jesus also says in Mathew 28:18 (NKJ), **"All authority has been given to Me in heaven and on earth. Go therefore."**

Jesus is telling us that we have the same authority He does in Heaven and on earth. Therefore, go and use His name to make disciples and to conquer and live the abundant life that Jesus speaks of. Jesus' name is the name that has power over every other name that is named above the earth, on the earth and below the earth (Phil. 2:9-10). So let that faith that is in you and every other born again believer work for you. Step forth boldly and use it! The battle is worth it. As you grow in God's Word and in boldness, you will come to the realization that the battles will never stop but victory in those battles is yours **every** time!

Speaking and Believing

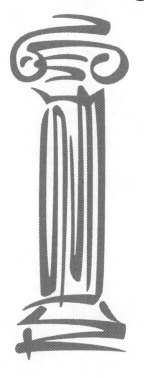

For assuredly, I say to you, whoever says to this mountain, 'Be removed and be cast into the sea,' and does not doubt in his heart, but believes that those things he says will be done, he will have whatever he says.

- Mark 11:23

Just Say It!

So what is the significance of 'saying?' It is to speak or confess God's Word over our circumstances instead of just whining and complaining and allowing doubt to lead us in how we respond to them.

I have friends and family who used to look at me funny or with raised eyebrows when I would tell them that I was not *confessing* something they were *speaking* but that I was only confessing what God and His Word had for me. I say 'used to' because they don't give us those looks any more after having witnessed the fruit in our lives.

I remember an instance with my mother, who was staying with us, and a cold I had contracted. I had come home from work and kept rebuking and speaking God's Word against it. My mom, who is a wonderful Christian woman, kept asking me if I was okay. I kept telling her I was fine and by Jesus' stripes I was healed. She wanted so badly for me to confess that I was sick and that I did not feel good. She just did not understand that for me to admit and speak such a thing would only add fuel to the affliction the Devil had put on me. Even though I was not going to deny that I was sick, I was only going to allow my mouth to say those things that I wanted to see come to pass.

She did not understand or believe the importance of *confessing* or *speaking* the right things.

God's Word says His people perish for lack of knowledge (Hosea 4:6). So often it is a lack of understanding or knowing what God's Word says about speaking His Word of faith that keeps people from doing it. Or, even worse, they are being taught the wrong things in their own church. Some church leaders just do not believe or are deceived about the power of our words.

My wife, Stephanie, and I visited a church a couple of years ago and began talking to a couple of people about the importance of speaking or having the right words come out of our mouth. The pastor of that church happened to overhear, and when we finished the conversation and began to walk away, he came up to us and quietly said, "Be careful, there's not that much power in your words." We were stunned. Here was the pastor, the leader of the people in this church, who sadly either did not know what God's Word says about what we confess or just chose not to believe it.

So what does God's word say about the power of our words? Right from the start, God's Word teaches us about using words to speak life into existence. I especially like the account of creation in the Message Bible. Read with me in Genesis chapter one:

3-5 God spoke: "Light!"
And light appeared.
God saw that light was good
and separated light from dark.

God named the light Day,
    he named the dark Night.
It was evening, it was morning—
Day One.

6-8 God spoke: "Sky! In the middle of the waters;
    separate water from water!"
God made sky.
He separated the water under sky
    from the water above sky.
And there it was:
    he named sky the Heavens;
It was evening, it was morning—
Day Two.

9-10 God spoke: "Separate!
    Water-beneath-Heaven, gather into one place;
Land, appear!"
    And there it was.
God named the land Earth.
    He named the pooled water Ocean.
God saw that it was good.

11-13 God spoke: "Earth, green up! Grow all varieties
    of seed-bearing plants,
Every sort of fruit-bearing tree."
    And there it was.
Earth produced green seed-bearing plants,
    all varieties,
And fruit-bearing trees of all sorts.
    God saw that it was good.
It was evening, it was morning—
Day Three.

14-15 God spoke: "Lights! Come out!
    Shine in Heaven's sky!
Separate Day from Night.
    Mark seasons and days and years,
Lights in Heaven's sky to give light to Earth."
    And there it was.

16-19 God made two big lights, the larger
    to take charge of Day,
The smaller to be in charge of Night;
    and he made the stars.
God placed them in the heavenly sky
    to light up Earth
And oversee Day and Night,
    to separate light and dark.
God saw that it was good.
It was evening, it was morning—
Day Four.

20-23 God spoke: "Swarm, Ocean, with fish and all sea life!
    Birds, fly through the sky over Earth!"
God created the huge whales,
    all the swarm of life in the waters,
And every kind and species of flying birds.
    God saw that it was good.
God blessed them: "Prosper! Reproduce! Fill Ocean!
    Birds, reproduce on Earth!"
It was evening, it was morning—
Day Five.

24-25 God spoke: "Earth, generate life! Every sort and kind:
    cattle and reptiles and wild animals—all kinds."

And there it was:
    wild animals of every kind,
Cattle of all kinds, every sort of reptile and bug.
    God saw that it was good.

26-28 God spoke: "Let us make human beings in our image…"

Notice, on every new day, God did something to bring things into existence. He spoke! He spoke light and it appeared. He spoke sky and it appeared. He spoke "generate life" and life appeared! God speaks things into existence. He spoke human beings into existence. God created us in His image, so what does that mean we should be doing? We need to be speaking things into existence! In Romans 4:17, God teaches us to speak of things that do not exist as though they do. Here is what it says:

"God, who gives life to the dead and calls those things which do not exist as though they did."

The Scripture here is speaking of Abraham, who God called the father of many nations. God changed Abraham's name from Abram to Abraham. Do you know what Abraham means? It literally means 'the father of many nations.' So every time someone called Abraham's name, they called him 'the father of many nations.' It was being spoken into existence.

I need to make a very important point here. Go back to Romans chapter 4 with me and look at verse 17 and 18 again.

"'I have made you a father of many nations,' in the presence of Him whom he believed—God, who gives life to the dead

and calls those things which do not exist as though they did; who, contrary to hope, in hope believed, so that he became the father of many nations, according to what was spoken, 'So shall your descendants be.'"

There is a word in these two verses that is vitally important to us if we are to receive what we are speaking for. It is the word *'believed.'* We have to believe what God's Word says and promises us. Abraham believed what God spoke to him and that made his faith strong so that **"He did not waver at the promise of God through unbelief, but was strengthened in faith" (Romans 4:20).**

We must believe what God's Word promises us! Earlier in this book, when I spoke on the subject of God's Word, I made the comment that unbelief is the single biggest hindrance for us as believers in receiving God's promises. I will be perfectly honest with you in saying that I also struggle with this. We all do. We are called believers but do we really believe? For some reason it is easy for us to believe in our salvation, but when it comes to believing for healing or restoration in relationships or breaking through a stronghold in our life, we fall short of believing it can happen.

Why is this? It comes down primarily to two things. I am not going to say that these are the only two reasons, but I believe they are the two biggest reasons for unbelief. First, I believe we are not in God's Word enough. We focus too much on the circumstances around us and not on what God's Word promises us. We do not utilize His Word as the sword of the Spirit that is made available to us (Ephesians 6:17). But, if we do not know what His Word holds for us, then how can we believe.

"My people are destroyed for lack of knowledge" (Hosea 4:6, KJV).

"So then faith comes by hearing, and hearing by the word of God" (Romans 10:17).

Unbelief could also equal disobedience. God shows us that these two words are very similar to each other in Hebrews 3:18-19:

"And to whom did He swear that they would not enter His rest, but to those who did not obey? So we see that they could not enter in because of unbelief."

Many people are educated in what the Bible tells us, but unfortunately, many of them are not educated beyond their level of obedience or belief.

The second reason that we don't believe is that once we know what God's Word says for us we speak contrary to it. So, we **must** know what God's Word promises us and we **must** speak words that line up with what He promises us. *Romans 10:8 says,* **"But what does it** (God's Word) **say? The word is near you, in your mouth and in your heart** (that is the Word of faith which we preach)."

How does the Word get near us? By reading it, studying it, meditating on it, and by hearing it taught to us. Then once we have it, we need to have it in our mouths, speaking it! *Verse 9 in Romans chapter 10* goes on to say, **"That if you confess with your mouth the Lord Jesus and believe in your heart that God raised Him from the dead, you will be saved."**

God spoke to me one day as I meditated on that verse and told me, "You know, I didn't give you that verse just to get you to Heaven. I gave you that verse so you could be saved from all the junk that the Devil and life in general has piled on you." I shared with you earlier in this book all that the word 'salvation' encompasses. We must get that knowledge planted firmly in our heads to truly understand what God is saying here to us.

Salvation brings us deliverance, aid, health, and welfare. In the Greek, it is the word '**soteria**' and literally means 'to rescue.' So what is God saying with this verse? He is saying is that we must be confessing with our mouth and believing in our hearts for any area of our lives that we need a breakthrough in or need to be rescued in. When we are speaking it, when we are confessing it, when we are saying it over and over and over, it will get into our hearts, we will begin to believe it, and it will come to pass in our lives!

Jesus put a whole lot of stock in believing. He is constantly, throughout the New Testament, encouraging and admonishing us to "only believe." In Ephesians 1:19, Paul prays that we may know **"...what is the exceeding greatness of His power toward us who believe according to the working of His mighty power which He worked in Christ when he raised Him from the dead...."**

In fact, the word 'believe' is mentioned in the bible 268 times and 226 of those times are in the New Testament! 118 of them are found in the first four books or the Gospels. The word 'unbelief' is mentioned 12 times and all of them are in the New Testament.

There are two times in the Bible that Jesus marveled. One time was in the account of the centurion who had a paralyzed and tormented servant. He said to Jesus, "**'I am not worthy that You should come under my roof. But only speak a word, and my servant will be healed'**" (Matt. 8:8, NKJ).

In verse 10 continues the story: "**When Jesus heard it, He marveled, and said to those who followed, 'Assuredly I say to you that I have not found such great faith, not even in Israel.'**"

So Jesus marveled at the faith of a man who was not even a Jew! The other time that Jesus marveled can be found in Mark 6:5-6:

"**Now He could do no mighty work there, except that He laid His hands on a few sick people and healed** *them. And He marveled because of their unbelief.* **Then He went about the villages in a circuit, teaching.**"

He marveled at their unbelief! Do you think that He does not do the same with us today? Jesus also rebuked their unbelief in Mark 16:14:

"**Later He appeared to the eleven as they sat at the table; and He rebuked their unbelief and hardness of heart, because they did not believe those who had seen Him after He had risen.**"

I believe the same thing is happening to us, myself included, today. Jesus is watching us and marveling at our unbelief. He watches us going about our lives, getting caught up in the cares of this world and focusing on our circumstances instead of God's Word. He sees us letting the wants and desires of our flesh cloud what we think or believe, ultimately putting a roadblock in front of what God is trying to get to us. Hebrews chapter 3 verses 12 and 13 give us a very good indication of how God views unbelief:

"Be careful then, dear brothers and sisters. Make sure that your own hearts are not evil and unbelieving, turning you away from the living God. You must warn each other every day, while it is still 'today,' so that none of you will be deceived by sin and hardened against God."

Make sure that your own hearts are not evil and unbelieving. God views an unbelieving heart the same as an evil heart that is deceived by sin!

I think one of the strongest verses on speaking and believing can be found in John 14:12-14 from the NKJ:

"Most assuredly, I say to you, he who believes in Me, the works that I do he will do also; and greater *works* than these he will do, because I go to My Father. And whatever you ask in My name, that I will do, that the Father may be glorified in the Son. If you ask anything in My name, I will do *it*."

It really can't be said any more clearly than that. Jesus said, 'most assuredly,' or 'certainly, without a doubt.' If we will only ask or say or **speak** and **believe,** we will have the things we ask for in His name, and not only that, but we will do greater things than He did. I really like how it is presented in the Amplified bible:

"I assure you, most solemnly I tell you, if anyone steadfastly believes in Me, he will himself be able to do the things that I do; and he will do even greater things than these, because I go to the Father. And I will do [I Myself will grant] **whatever you ask in My Name** [as presenting all that I AM], **so that the Father may be glorified and extolled in (through) the Son.** [Yes] **I will grant** [I Myself will do for you] **whatever you shall ask in My Name** [as presenting all that I AM]."**

I'll bet I read over this verse 20 or 30 times before I came to an understanding or, better yet, a **belief** of what it is saying. Once I did, I began believing for and asking for all kinds of things. I began believing and asking for ways to get out of debt. I began believing for a new car. I began believing for health and restoration in my body where it was needed. I began speaking for all those things and confessing that they were mine. At this point, I could go on and say that God granted all those things and that life was just wonderful with absolutely no problems. But, if I did that, I would be lying.

Yes, God did open my eyes up to what His Word was saying in John chapter 14, but just like any good father, He did not just begin lavishing things upon me. As parents, we would never put our 5 year-old child behind the wheel of our car and say, "There you go, have a good time." No, we protect our children, and as they are ready for certain things, we allow them into their lives. It is no different with God. As we mature in our walk with and love for Him and as His Word grows in our hearts, we are brought to a place where He can do great works through us and in us.

God uses His Word, the Holy Spirit, and other people to bring wisdom into our lives. He also makes it very clear in His Word that He is not going to give us responsibility over much, if we are not responsible over little. God is going to protect us and He is going to protect His kingdom. If something is going to keep His kingdom from advancing or **Him being glorified,** no matter how much we may want it, then He is not going to do it for us. Let me give you a couple of examples from my own life.

Several years ago, when I was really beginning to understand what God's Word held for us in the area of healing, I injured my back. Healing came to me in a spectacular and cool way. Here is what happened. I was working in our basement, and as I bent over to grab a board, my lower back just popped. I went right to my knees. It hurt so bad I had tears in my eyes. I was also mad, because it was not anything heavy that I had tried to lift. I couldn't understand why my back would give out. I had never had any trouble with my back before. But that is just how the Devil works.

My wife and I were at a point in our lives where we were really learning and believing what God's Word said for us about living a healthy and prosperous life—especially in the area of our health. There were things going on in our lives in the area of our health that, according to God's Word, just should not be happening. It seemed like we were sick all the time, either myself or Stephanie or one of the boys—sometimes all of us would be sick at the same time! We had bought into what everyone else had also bought into who didn't really know what God's Word promised. We figured we just had to live with being sick and that it was just a part of life. If we got around other people who were sick, then we were going to get sick too. That is not what God's Word says for us though. His Word in Psalm 91:10 says, **"There shall no evil befall thee, neither shall any plague come nigh thy dwelling."**

In other words, no sickness is going to come into our home! In verse four He says that He will cover us with His feathers and under His wings we shall take refuge. He is saying He will protect us no matter where we go! Jesus paid the price for us not to have to be sick. Isaiah 53:4-5 says this:

**"Surely He has borne our griefs
    And carried our sorrows;
    Yet we esteemed Him stricken,
    Smitten by God, and afflicted.
    But He *was* wounded for our transgressions,
    He was bruised for our iniquities;
    The chastisement for our peace *was* upon Him,
    And by His stripes we are healed."**

We began to understand that if we would live our lives completely for Jesus Christ and believe what His Word promised us, we did not have to live in sickness and in sorrow any more. The words 'grief' and 'sorrows' in the verse above literally mean **'pain'** and **'sickness.'** Jesus carried that away from us, and it does not belong in us at all anymore! The word 'peace' in verse five translated in Hebrew means 'good health, prosperity and favor.' That is what Jesus did for us! He broke the Devil's back. He redeemed us from the curse, having become a curse for us (Gal. 3:13). The chastisement, or correction and discipline, for our **peace** was upon Him! We really began to get this.

We did not have to live life that way anymore, so naturally, the enemy attacked, and of course, the attack came in the area of health. And not having won enough battles, doubt and unbelief came in immediately. My back was killing me, literally. I hurt it on a Saturday morning and by Sunday night I was convinced I was going to have to see a doctor about it. I laid around moping and forgetting everything I had just learned in God's Word. Then God brought a very special person to wake me up. That very special person was my son Tristan who was 5 years old at the time. He came up to me on Sunday night while I kind of laid there moaning and said, "Daddy, are you okay?" I answered, "My back just really hurts, buddy. I think I am going to have to miss work tomorrow and go see the doctor." His answer hit me like a wakeup call. He said, "Well, we just need to pray for it, daddy. Jesus will heal it." Well duh, I thought. Why hadn't I done that already? Because I was focusing on my circumstances and speaking the wrong things and letting self-pity take over.

It is amazing how God takes the simple, or childlike, things of the world to wake us up sometimes. So my son put his little hands on my lower back and he prayed. It was a very simple prayer. He said, "Thank you Jesus for healing daddy's back." Then I agreed with him that my back **was** healed. It was already done. Now it didn't happen right that moment. My back still hurt, but I was standing on that little prayer and remembering what God's word said for me. So I went to bed that night with my back still really hurting, and I finally drifted off to sleep.

I actually slept. The night before, I didn't get hardly any sleep. The next morning I got up and started getting ready for work. I was through my shower and halfway through shaving before it hit me! My back didn't hurt anymore! I bent over and twisted around. I felt great. That was a huge moment in my faith walk. From that moment I walked, confessed, and taught my family and myself that we live in divine health! In the past several years, we have had plenty of times that sickness has come upon us, but we confess God's Word against it immediately, and it never lasts.

I had a different experience with my eyes. I had been wearing glasses for a couple of years, and when we came to the revelation of living in divine health, I began to confess that my eyes were healed. I thanked God every day that I could see perfectly, and I did began to see a difference—but not enough that I would quit wearing my glasses or contacts. I began to wear them less like not putting them on over the weekends or on vacation. Then one day, as I went to put my contacts in, I heard God speak to me through my spirit, and He said, "Mark, every time you put those contacts in, you take away the healing that is there for you." I was stunned. I had never thought of it that way, and I made the decision to walk by faith and not by sight (literally!).

Now, there was not an immediate complete healing. Over a period of time, my eyes got better and better, and after about six months or so, I realized my eyesight was nearly perfect. I was able to go anywhere and do anything and see without any problem at all.

Let me make something very clear here. I would never recommend to someone to stop taking a prescribed medication or to stop wearing glasses unless they knew, without a doubt, that they had heard from God. On the other side of that, when you hear God, you better believe and not doubt or your opportunity will be lost.

Now, there have been other times when I have prayed for things and believed for them and have never seen them come to pass. I remember one time where I was believing for a new car. It was this one particular car that I just really wanted, and since Stephanie and I had sown several cars to others, I believed we were going to have it. I never got it. At least it hasn't shown up yet! But I believe the reason God has not granted me that car is because I was letting pride come into my life due to the cars we had sown in the past. God knew that my heart and my maturity level were not ready for receiving this kind of gift from Him. I am thankful that God could see this even when I could not. Notice, that I said the new car has not shown up **yet**. I fully expect it to. You might ask me why I expect this to happen and my answer would be because God's Word says it will. Look with me at what it says in Galatians 6:7-9:

"Do not be deceived, God is not mocked; for whatever a man sows, that he will also reap. For he who sows to his flesh will of the flesh reap corruption, but he who sows to the Spirit will of the Spirit reap everlasting life. And let us not grow weary while doing good, for in due season we shall reap if we do not lose heart."

I love what that says. God will not be mocked. **Whatever** we sow we will also reap. And then He goes on to say not to grow weary while doing good. If we will be patient, we will reap if we don't lose heart. So I am not going to grow weary while doing good. We may give another car away before we see the one I believe is coming. That is where the joy is anyway. It is in the giving and in walking in obedience to what God is asking us to do.

I really don't care if we ever get a new car given to us, but I know, according to God's Word, that it **will** happen. That is, if we keep believing. This is what God means when He tells us **not to lose heart**. He is saying, "Don't stop believing!" Believing is so important. How do we keep believing? I'm glad you asked. I know I have said this often in this book, but it takes staying in God's Word every day. It takes praying and fasting and listening to good biblical teaching that is available to us. It takes making Jesus Christ Lord over every part of our lives!

Confessing and Believing
will Remove Mountains

When it comes to confessing and believing, Jesus taught it best in Mark chapter 11:20-26. I know many of you may be familiar with this teaching in the Bible, but I want to take a renewed and closer look at what Jesus is saying here. We need to look at Mark chapter 11 starting with verse 12:

"Now the next day, when they had come out from Bethany, He was hungry. And seeing from afar a fig tree having leaves, He went to see if perhaps He would find something on it. When He came to it, He found nothing but leaves, for it was not the season for figs. In response Jesus said to it, 'Let no one eat fruit from you ever again.' And His disciples heard *it*."

We need to understand that, just like any of us, Jesus had a need. He was hungry. So, seeing the fig tree with many leaves, He decided to go get some figs. During the spring when the leaves are developing on fig trees, the figs are normally developing right along with them. This particular tree did not do this. Now, if this had been many of us, we probably would have whined and complained about it, saying, "I just knew there wouldn't be anything on this tree. Why did I waste my time coming over here? What am I going to do now? How am I ever going to overcome this problem?" Instead, Jesus just decided that if this tree was not going to be fruitful, then no one would ever deal with it again.

So He said to it, "Let no one eat fruit from you ever again." We know that He spoke it out loud, because the next sentence says, "And His disciples heard it." So, we learn here that we need to speak to our problems, needs, and circumstances **out loud**. Jesus goes on to teach even more of this in verses 20-26:

"Now in the morning, as they passed by, they saw the fig tree dried up from the roots. And Peter, remembering, said to Him, 'Rabbi, look! The fig tree which You cursed has withered away.'

So Jesus answered and said to them, 'Have faith in God. For assuredly, I say to you, whoever says to this mountain, 'Be removed and be cast into the sea,' and does not doubt in his heart, but believes that those things he says will be done, he will have whatever he says. Therefore I say to you, whatever things you ask when you pray, believe that you receive *them*, and you will have *them*.'"

Now, we need to take a close look at this. Break these verses down and you will see that Jesus gave us a four step plan on **How to Move Problems out of Our Lives.** This may sound silly, but it is really true. Verse 22 gives us the first step. Jesus says to them, "Have faith in God." We have to have **faith in God.** Personally, I believe that Jesus was almost shouting this at them in exasperation. It was only a couple of chapters earlier in chapter 9 that we read:

"Jesus said to them, 'You faithless people! How long must I be with you? How long must I put up with you'" (Mark 9:19)?

Ouch! That had to have hurt. But how often are we the same way? We have problems or circumstances come into our lives, and instead of addressing them the way that Jesus addressed the fig tree, we wallow around in self pity, whining and complaining instead of letting our faith speak to the problem. We have to understand that we **must** have faith in God—not in ourselves, not in other people, not in money or any other thing. Our faith has to be in God and God alone! We all make mistakes, and we all have trials and tribulations come into our lives, but we need to have the attitude of David as he says in Psalms 21:6:

"Now I know that the LORD saves His anointed;
He will answer him from His holy heaven
With the saving strength of His right hand."

If you have made Jesus Christ the Lord of your life, then you are His anointed! Galations 3:29 tells us, **"And if you _are_ Christ's, then you are Abraham's seed, and heirs according to the promise."**

If we can fully understand this, we will have faith in God, and we will be well on our way to overcoming whatever problem it is that we are facing in our lives. To have faith in God, we must know what His Word says. We must be reading it and hearing it daily. Romans 10:17 says, **"So then faith _comes_ by hearing, and hearing by the word of God."**

So our faith is strengthened by hearing the good news of God's Word, the Message of what Jesus Christ did for us on the day of redemption.

The second step in overcoming a problem or circumstance is that we need to **be speaking to it**. This does not just mean having positive thoughts in our head, but we need to be speaking *out loud* to our problem. Jesus says in Mark 11:23, **"For assuredly, I say to you, whoever says to this mountain, 'Be removed and be cast into the sea…'"**

Whenever Jesus uses the word 'assuredly' to begin a sentence, He is trying to get our attention. The word 'assuredly' translated from the Greek is the word *'amen'* and means: surely, truly, of a truth, so it is, or so be it. In effect, Jesus is saying, "You really need to listen to this!" We need to be **speaking** to our mountain and our mountain is, of course, the problem or circumstance we are facing in our lives. Jesus shows us in verse 14 that He spoke out loud to the fig tree and it listened to Him. If we look at the rest of verse 23 in Mark chapter 11 (KJV), we will notice that Jesus uses the word 'says' three times in that one verse.

"For assuredly, I say to you, whoever says to this mountain, 'Be removed and be cast into the sea,' and does not doubt in his heart, but believes that those things he says will be done, he will have whatever he says."

So, whoever "says" to their mountain will find that those things he "says" will be done. He will have whatever he "says." I can't say it any clearer than that. If we have arthritis, we need to say, "Arthritis, in the name of Jesus, get out of my body and be cast into the sea." If we are having trouble in our marriage we need to wake up every morning and say, "I have a wonderful marriage and a wonderful spouse. Thank you, God, that You are going to help me love my spouse the way You taught us to in Your Word...regardless of what I am seeing right now." Please notice the last part of that sentence. Jesus never said to speak to your mountain only after you see some results.

When God first got a hold of my heart, causing me to truly begin to live for Him, I wanted so badly for my wife, Stephanie, to be right there beside me. However, partly due to the hurt I had caused her before I got saved, she was finding it difficult to commit herself to seeking God with the passion that I was showing.

Now, let me show you the wrong thing to do. I asked her every day, "Did you take time to read your Bible and pray?" After she responded in the negative, I would quote verses to her about why it is important to have God's Word in our hearts. This only pushed her further away from where I desired her to be, and quite honestly, it confused me.

So I spent some time praying and asking God what I needed to do, and He spoke to me through a good friend. My friend said, "Mark, you need to love her where she is at and then pray and thank God for the desire that is growing inside of her to seek Him passionately." So I began to do just that. I loved on her and tried to find extra little things I could do for her, and then, every morning, I praised God for the fire that was igniting in her heart to know Him and to seek Him. I did this for almost two years before I saw a change in her desire to seek God. It was like a switch turned on! All of a sudden, she was reading her Bible and praying and asking me and other people questions about what God's Word says. I really believe (and Stephanie will say she does too) that it was due to my daily speaking, praying and praising God for the results that I desired to see.

Jesus told us we will have whatever we say. Knowing this, we must learn or train ourselves to be speaking the positive things we desire to see and not the negative thoughts that are often driven into our heads due the circumstances we may be facing. Let me give you a couple of examples.

A lady came to my wife and me about her troubles with her 12 year old son. She was very concerned about his speech and actions around other girls his age and somewhat older than he. She had also caught him looking at some pornography and was having a hard time keeping control of him. Her words to us at that time were, "I just know he is going to get himself into a lot of trouble if we can't get some control over this." Even her words to her son about this issue were negative—speaking negative words into him that were contrary to the results she really wanted to see.

Stephanie immediately told her to begin speaking those things that she desired for and believed in and not the things that she was seeing. Romans 4:17 says to speak of the non-existent things as though they exist. The best way to do that is to take it right to God's Word. We showed what God's Word says in Isaiah 54:13(NKJ):

"All your children *shall be* taught by the LORD, And great *shall be* the peace of your children."

And also what Psalms 112:1-3(NLT, italics added) says:

1 Praise the LORD!
   How joyful are those who fear the LORD
      and delight in obeying his commands.
2 *Their children* **will be successful everywhere;**
      an entire generation of godly people will be blessed.
3 They themselves will be wealthy,
      and their good deeds will last forever.

We need to find out what God's Word says for every *mountain* in our lives and then begin speaking those words over it and begin telling that mountain to get out of our lives and be cast into the sea forever!

That lady began doing what God's Word told her to do and, within two weeks, came back to us to report that she already saw a difference in her son's actions. At that point, we also began to work with her on *why* she had spoken the negative things she had said. Also, we addressed *why* her son had been doing some of the things he had been doing. This leads us to the next question we must all ask ourselves.

What are we allowing into our lives? Are we watching the news constantly? I believe that watching the news can be one of the worst things we can be doing when it comes to trying to think and speak positively. It does little but pump doom and gloom into our heads and our hearts. If our kids are sitting there next to us, it is even worse for them. They have their whole lives ahead of them, and if they are hearing all the junk about the economy failing, crime on the rise, and new diseases popping up all over, what kind of hope are they going to have? What are we putting in our hearts? If junk is the only thing going in, then junk is the only thing that is going to come out. Jesus teaches this in Matthew 12:34-37:

"For whatever is in your heart determines what you say. A good person produces good things from the treasury of a good heart, and an evil person produces evil things from the treasury of an evil heart. And I tell you this, you must give an account on judgment day for every idle word you speak. The words you say will either acquit you or condemn you."

Jesus makes it very clear here. **Every** word we speak is directly connected to what we are putting into our hearts, and every word we speak not only affects us now (we will have whatever we say!), but will also affect us on judgment day. We will either be justified by what we say or we will be condemned! If we fill our hearts with God's Word and His teachings, we really begin to understand that faith comes by hearing and hearing by the Word of God. Only then we will begin to speak the right things and gain a boldness that the Devil cannot withstand!

Jesus said we will have what we say, that our words will either acquit us or condemn us. So what are we saying? When we get around someone with the flu are we saying, "Oh great, now I am going to get the flue too?" I suggest saying, "In the name of Jesus that cold will not touch me! I have been redeemed from the curse of sickness (Galatians 3:13). The redeeming blood of Christ flows through this body and sickness has no authority over it!" You will have what you say! So begin to speak what you want and let those words begin to replace the negative feelings and thoughts that are in your heart. The Word is near me, in my mouth and in my heart (Romans 10:8).

The third step in this process is to **believe and not doubt.**

"I tell you the truth, you can say to this mountain, 'May you be lifted up and thrown into the sea,' and it will happen. But you must really believe it will happen and have no doubt in your heart" (Mark 11:23, NLT).

Not only must we speak to our mountain, but we must believe it will happen and have *no* doubt in our hearts, none, no doubt at all. I taught earlier in this section about unbelief, and I am going make this statement again: I think unbelief is the single biggest hindrance that people face when trying to overcome adverse situations in their lives. This is especially true in America. Let me give you an example.

Recently, our church sent a team to the Philippians on a mission trip. This was truly a trip to carry out the commission given to us by Christ in Mark chapter 16 to, "Go into the world and preach the gospel to every creature." This team went, truly believing in what Jesus says next in these last few verses of the book of Mark (KJV):

"And He said to them, 'Go into all the world and preach the gospel to every creature. 16 He who believes and is baptized will be saved; but he who does not believe will be condemned. 17 And these signs will follow those who believe: In My name they will cast out demons; they will speak with new tongues; 18 they[b] will take up serpents; and if they drink anything deadly, it will by no means hurt them; they will lay hands on the sick, and they will recover.'"

This team went to the Philippians, fully expecting to do all of these, and the results were exactly what we <u>should</u> expect everywhere we go. While they were there, almost 7,000 natives received Jesus Christ as their Savior. These people were also taught the truth about how God did not desire to see them living in sickness, and there were over 3,700 confirmed healings, including everything from blind eyes being opened to the lame and crippled walking and goiters disappearing from bodies. As we heard the testimonies from the people who went on the trip, the people in our church listened with joy and amazement. There were also many people asking this question, "Why were so many people there healed yet so many people here struggle with being healed?" I won't say that the answer lies in any one thing, but I do believe that much of the reason can be found in Mark chapter 4 where Jesus teaches us on the parable of the sower.

"13 And He said to them, "Do you not understand this parable? How then will you understand all the parables? 14 The sower sows the word. 15 And these are the ones by the wayside where the word is sown. When they hear, Satan comes immediately and takes away the word that was sown in their hearts. 16 These likewise are the ones sown on stony ground who, when they hear the word, immediately receive it with gladness; 17 and they have no root in themselves, and so endure only for a time. Afterward, when tribulation or persecution arises for the word's sake, immediately they stumble. 18 Now these are the ones sown among thorns; *they are* the ones who hear the word, 19 and the cares of this world, the deceitfulness of riches, and the desires for other things entering in "choke the word, and it becomes unfruitful. 20 But these are the ones sown on good ground, those who hear

the word, accept *it,* and bear fruit: some thirtyfold, some sixty, and some a hundred."

While all of these verses give us reasons that can affect our walk of faith, I want to give special attention to verse 18 and 19. "*Now these are the ones sown among thorns; they are the ones who hear the word, and the cares of this world, the deceitfulness of riches, and the desires for other things entering in choke the word, and it becomes unfruitful.*" Look at the word 'they' that I have underlined in that verse. Like it or not, try and deny it if you like, but that word represents, in part, the people of the United States of America. The Devil has used the media and our society in general to turn us into a society of "what about me, what about me, what about me!" As believers, we are fed God's Word. *The sower sows the Word,* but we have let these three things mentioned here in God's Word drive doubt and unbelief deep into our hearts, denying us from seeing the fruit that God truly desires for us to see in our lives. These three things are again:

1. The cares of this world.
2. The deceitfulness of riches, running after the almighty dollar.
3. The desires for other things, a lie planted inside of us that we need more and more stuff.

People in third world countries have not had their hearts clouded with all the garbage that is so generously spooned out to us here in the United States or any other country that has forgotten that it is God that has given them the ability to acquire wealth (Deuteronomy 8:18). People in these third world countries simply have hearts that are more open to receive and believe what is taught to them about God's Word (**Mark 4:24-25).**

So, back to the third step that Jesus is teaching us here in Mark chapter 11. To experience a fruitful life in God's Word, we **must** not doubt in our heart, but believe what we say will be done. Then we will have whatever we say.

How do we get to this point of total belief with no doubt in our heart? Without God's help, it is impossible to do this. Even with it, we will struggle because the Devil will never stop trying to convince us that moving our problem mountain is impossible. But it can be moved, and we do it like this:

First of all, we saturate ourselves in God's Word and we <u>must</u> believe without compromise what God's Word says. Secondly, we must live by what God's Word says, again, without compromise. We must seek Him and desire His 'presence' more that any 'thing' He can give us. Thirdly, we have got to be speaking the right things. In Isaiah 57:18-19 (NKJ), God speaks to us about how He will give us the things we should speak and how it will bring peace into our lives. Look at what it says:

> **"I have seen his ways, and will heal him;**
> **I will also lead him,**
> **And restore comforts to him**
> **And to his mourners.**
> **I create the fruit of the lips:**
>> **Peace, peace to *him who is* far off and to *him who is* near,"**
>> **Says the LORD,**
> **And I will heal him."**

God creates the fruit of our lips. He gave us the words we need to speak! It is His Word! We need to be praising Him according to what His Word says as well as speaking and believing the promises He has there for us. As we continually speak it, we will begin to believe it in our heart. Proverbs 23:7 (NKJ) says; **"For as he thinks in his heart, so is he."**

When we begin to think and live and speak this way, we will have the peace that God promises in Isaiah 57:19. That word 'peace' in this verse, when translated in the Hebrew, means *to be well and happy, to have good health, prosperity and favour, and to be whole.* That promise is there for *us.*

Jesus teaches us in John 14:14 that if we ask what God has promised, in Jesus name, He will do it. It says this, **"If you ask anything in My name, I will do *it.*"**

It says anything. Not *some* things, but _anything_ that lines up with God's Word and His promises.

The fourth step that Jesus gives us to move the mountains in our lives **concerns taking offense and giving forgiveness.** Taking offense and holding un-forgiveness in our hearts contributes largely to why people do not either see themselves drawing closer to God or see their lives improving. Mark 11:25-26 (NLT) says this:

"But when you are praying, first forgive anyone you are holding a grudge against, so that your Father in heaven will forgive your sins, too."

It is so easy to take offense and have un-forgiveness in our hearts, but Jesus makes it very clear that if we don't forgive, then God is not going to forgive us, nor will He answer those prayers or words that we are lifting up to Him for help. When it comes right down to it, we are not walking in the love that I talked about earlier in this book. If you remember, Paul tells us in chapter 13 of 1 Corinthians that it does not matter what we are doing or how good we do it. If we are not doing it out of love, it means nothing. Here is what it says:

"1 If I could speak all the languages of earth and of angels, but didn't love others, I would only be a noisy gong or a clanging cymbal. 2 If I had the gift of prophecy, and if I understood all of God's secret plans and possessed all knowledge, and if I had such faith that I could move mountains, but didn't love others, I would be nothing. 3 If I gave everything I have to the poor and even sacrificed my body, I could boast about it; but if I didn't love others, I would have gained nothing."

When we are harboring offense and un-forgiveness in our hearts, then we are not operating in love, and when we are not operating in love, faith cannot work in our lives because we know that faith works by love (Galatians 5:6).

It is really kind of funny—or at least strange—how we often think when we are upset with what someone has done to us. We think to ourselves, "Well, I'm not going to talk to them anymore," or "I'm just not going to be very nice to them when I see them." We think that in doing this, we are getting back at them and that it will make us feel better. In reality, it just allows a root of bitterness to grow inside, hardening our hearts and putting up a wall between us and God. These kinds of actions are like taking a knife, sticking it in our own heart, and then expecting the other person to die from it!

Jesus tells us that we must forgive our brothers or sisters, not just once or twice, but repeatedly, over and over. He says it this way in Mathew 18 (NKJ):

"21 Then Peter came to Him and said, 'Lord, how often shall my brother sin against me, and I forgive him? Up to seven times?'

22 Jesus said to him, 'I do not say to you, up to seven times, but up to seventy times seven.'"

Jesus then goes on to tell a story about a man who was in debt to his king, and the king decided that he wanted all his servants to settle their debts to him—immediately. Now this man owed a great deal to the king, and having no means to pay back his debt, the king determined to sell the man and his family into slavery to make payment for the debt. The man begged with the king to have mercy, promising to work very hard to pay back all that he owed. The king was moved with compassion and not only released the man from prison, but forgave him the entire debt. This man then went out and grabbed a person who owed him a much smaller debt and had this poor man thrown in prison because he could not pay what he owed either. When the king heard of this, he found the man who he had forgiven and had him bound and thrown to the torturers.

Jesus made it clear that this is what would happen to us if we would not forgive our brothers and sisters their sin against us. He says it this way in Matthew 18:35:

"So My heavenly Father also will do to you if each of you, from his heart, does not forgive his brother his trespasses."

Forgiveness is not an option. It is something that must be done if we desire to see those mountains in our lives removed and cast into the sea!

Thus far, we have learned about the first three pillars of faith: God's Word, Love, and Speaking and Believing. With each if these, as I have said repeatedly throughout this book, it takes daily effort in seeking God through His Word, in prayer and good biblical teaching. It also takes both a genuine, heart-felt desire to know Jesus Christ intimately as a friend would and to trust Him with every part of your life.

In the last section of this book, we are going to find out what the last pillar of faith is. It is one that I—and many others—struggle with. It truly goes hand in hand with faith when you look at it in terms of the laws and powers of God. Please, read on to find out what it is!

Patience

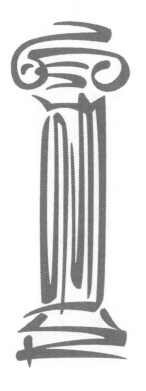

"God's way of answering the Christian's prayer for more patience, experience, hope and love often is to put him into the furnace of affliction."

Richard Cecil

Microwave or Blessing?

I chuckled as my son performed several tricks with a yoyo. "You are really getting good on that thing," I said. "Pretty soon you will be a yoyo master!"

"Thanks Dad," he replied. "But Dad, I really want that Duncan Dragonfly yoyo that they showed us at school. I could do a lot more tricks on it. Can we please go to the toy store downtown and see if they have any? One of my friends at school told me the store has them even cheaper than what they were selling them at school."

So off we went to the toy store with Corbin talking non-stop about all the cool things he would be able to do with his new yoyo. When we arrived at the store, we slowly made our way to the area where the yoyos were sold, all the while looking at the cool things that lined the shelves and hung from the ceilings. For a person like me—who is really still a kid stuck inside the body of a full grown man—the toy store was one of the coolest places to go!

When we got to the area that the yoyo's were kept in, it only took a quick look to see that the one Corbin wanted was out of stock. We talked to the owner of the store, and he quickly assured us that he would have more of that model next week. Corbin looked longingly at the wall where the yoyo's hung and said, "Dad, here is another one I could buy. Do you think I should get it?"

I took a look at the yoyo, and while it seemed pretty cool, it was almost twice the cost of the one Corbin really wanted. "Corbin," I said, "I think you should wait and get the one you really want."

"But Dad, I really want to get a good yoyo today," he said.

"I know buddy," I replied. "I still think it would be wise to wait. If you do, you are going to save money, and you will get the yoyo you really want."

Corbin nodded reluctantly and said, "I guess God is trying to help me learn about patience today, huh Dad?"

"Buddy, I think God tries to teach all of us patience every day!" I replied with a grin.

In this last part of looking at the 'Four Pillars to Strengthen our Faith,' I want to talk about something our society, including many who go to church, have made nearly non-existent and that is *patience*, or longsuffering, or waiting upon God to move in a situation. In the story above, Corbin learned, hopefully, the benefits of being patient and waiting patiently for what is promised. For him, it was the benefit of having something he really wanted at a lower price. For us, it may mean waiting patiently for God to move in difficult circumstances while enduring them, sometimes painfully.. Patience is believing that God is going to bring something great out of difficult circumstances. The hard part for us is that it is in Him timing, not in ours!

This kind of enduring or patient waiting does not happen very much anymore. We live in a microwave society of 'I want all and I want it now!' We live in a world that puts it on credit to have it now instead of waiting until there is the cash to pay for it. We impatiently force our way through a situation instead of waiting on what God is trying to bring to us through it. I am just as guilty! I get impatient when I don't think people do things the way they should be done. I stand and stare at water, thinking that maybe it will boil faster if my laser eyes are boring into it. I jump all over Stephanie and our sons when I don't think they are moving fast enough when we are getting ready to go somewhere. We are all guilty of it in different areas of our lives.

And while impatience may seem worse—and probably is—in this era that we live in, we are not the first to be impatient when things are not going the way we think they should be. In the Old Testament, the Israelites grumbled and complained because things were not happening fast enough or happening the way they thought it should. As a result, they regularly grumbled and complained to Moses. Here is just one example found in Exodus chapter 17 and verse two:

"So once more the people complained against Moses. 'Give us water to drink!' they demanded. 'Quiet!' Moses replied. 'Why are you complaining against me? And why are you testing the LORD?'"

Instead of trusting God to provide for them and waiting patiently for Him to move, the Israelites decide to complain. Even though they had watched God perform miracles over and over again, they still found the need to complain. But God, in His amazing mercy and patience, provided what they needed despite their complaints. Instead of trusting in the Lord, they tested Him. Instead of patiently waiting upon Him to provide for them, they grumbled and murmured. Sound familiar? How many of us, myself included, have done the same thing? We get in the middle of something difficult or painful or find ourselves in a place of uncertainty and rather than waiting upon God and seeking Him, we begin to head off in a direction that we think is best or, like the Israelites, we complain against God or the people He has put in authority around us.

As Christians, we must understand that all of us will go through these difficult seasons in our lives. It is not a question of 'if' but 'when' these situations will come. And how we decide to deal with it can literally mean the difference between life and death. Let me give you an example from God's word.

In Exodus 32, Moses went up on the mountain to meet with God and remained there for a long time. Now there may be times when you think you sit through a *long* meeting of one sort or another, but no meeting I have ever attended compares to the length of this meeting Moses had. Moses met with God for 40 days and 40 nights. After a time, the Israelites became impatient and began to wonder if Moses was even coming back. Even though Moses had told them where he was going and what he was doing, they still questioned. Look at what it says in verse 1 of Exodus 32:

"Now when the people saw that Moses delayed coming down from the mountain, the people gathered together to Aaron, and said to him, 'Come, make us gods that shall go before us; for [as for] this Moses, the man who brought us up out of the land of Egypt, we do not know what has become of him.'"

Amazing! They had been told where Moses was going and what he was doing, yet they claimed not to have known what become of him. Granted, he was gone for some time, but he was with God! This lack of patience on the part of the Israelites nearly cost them their lives. This is what the Lord says in verse 9 of Exodus 32:

"And the LORD said to Moses, 'I have seen this people, and indeed it [is] a stiff-necked people! Now therefore, let Me alone, that My wrath may burn hot against them and I may consume them.'"

If you read on it is only through the pleadings of Moses that God spares the lives of the Israelites.

God is Longsuffering

As you can see, patience is something that man has battled against for thousands of years and our amazing God has been longsuffering in His actions towards us. There have been times that God has talked to me or showed me something I should do, and though I would usually start well, I found that as time went on and I did not see the results I thought should be happening, I would basically do what the Israelites did and begin to seek my own ways. It never ends well!

I am going to share with you one of the worst examples of this in my life. Several years ago, Stephanie and I were living in a small modular home and felt like God was speaking to us to look for a home that had more room and would be a better place to begin raising our children. We had just had our first son at the time and were expecting our second. We began looking and found some homes that would be a good investment but, for one reason or another, would not work out. I knew in my heart that God was leading us to purchase an older home that would not be too expensive, but after a period of time, we became impatient and decided to purchase some land and put a new home on it.

We found some land and had problems in the purchase of it—that should have been our first clue. But we put our heads down, ignoring the warning signs, and pushed ahead. Our pastor even tried to warn us. "Mark," he said, "I believe I am supposed to warn you about going forward with this house. I think it would be better if you tried to find something that was easier and less expensive."

But of course I thought I knew what I was doing and ignored his advice. I think my friend knew that God was going to call us into the ministry in a few years. Perhaps he knew that this house was going to become a hindrance. We ran into problem after problem in building the home, and it cost us much more than expected. To make a long story short—or at least shorter—we finally got into the home when our boys were 1½ and 3 years old.

We spent 6 years in that home and have some great memories. The Lord blessed us during this time, and we became more and more involved in the ministry. We came to know that He had a call on our lives, and so we began to try and sell the house. We didn't realize until that moment how upside down we were on our mortgage. The housing market had really begun to slide and the numbers did not look good for us.

Suddenly, I was offered a position in a church, but we were not sure what to do about the house. We prayed, "God, if this is something you want us to do, then open that door quickly, but if not, then close it." Within a couple of days, we had a young family ask us if we would consider a Lease with Purchase option for our home. They had a large down payment, and after praying about it and seeking other counsel, we decided to do it. We made the move and settled into full time ministry. We found a great home for a great price in the area we moved to and it seemed that all was going well. We had done a 2 year lease with purchase option on our old home and for about 14 months, things seemed to be going along great.

Then the lease payments began coming in late. We spoke with the couple, and they said they were struggling with finding work but thought they would be able to keep up if we were patient. Well, the payments stopped coming in all together, and we tried to make payments for a short time on both homes but just could not do it. We tried to do a short sale on the home, but the bank would not work with us. The bank finally foreclosed on the home and sold it in an auction, taking less than a short sale would have!

The bank then proceeded to sue us for the remaining balance. We could not pay. With my salary as a pastor, we just did not have the money to pay, and rather than risk putting us in trouble in other areas financially, we made the decision to declare bankruptcy. This was very, very hard for me. We had worked hard to get our financial standing to where it was, and these turn of events were devastating.

But, looking back, I realized it was our own fault. If we had been more patient and listened in the beginning, we would not have built that house and would not have ended up in the position we were in. Because of our lack of patience it did not end well. It is all done now and in the past, but it was a hard lesson learned. We are so thankful that God was longsuffering with us!

Patience Takes Strength
and Courage

Faith and patience are a powerful combination. It takes faith sometimes just to be patient, and so often, it is when we wait patiently that we will see our faith work. All through God's Word, we see examples of men and women that understood the importance of waiting patiently upon the Lord, trusting that He was going to come through.

David is an amazing example of this as demonstrated in many of the Psalms he wrote. Time after time, David speaks of the difficulties in his life and of the attacks on him physically, mentally and spiritually. But just as often, he speaks of God coming through for him...*if* he was willing to **wait**. Psalm 27:13-14 are two of my life verses and are ones I have leaned upon many times during difficult situations. Here is what they say:

"¹³*I would have lost heart,* **unless I had believed**
> **That I would see the goodness of the LORD**
> **In the land of the living.**

"¹⁴**Wait on the LORD;**
> **Be of good courage,**

**And He shall strengthen your heart;
Wait, I say, on the LORD!"**

David shows us three important things in these verses that I really want you to get. Sometimes we read over verses and while they warm our hearts or make us feel good, we are not seeing the meat that is really in them. At some point in our Christian lives, we have to move away from suckling on milk and begin to chew on real food, whole food...you know...steak! Paul talks about this in Hebrews 5:13-14:

"For everyone who partakes *only* of milk *is* unskilled in the word of righteousness, for he is a babe. But solid food belongs to those who are of full age, *that is*, those who by reason of use have their senses exercised to discern both good and evil."

God is showing us that, at some point in our Christian walk, we must begin to show a level of maturity that lifts us above the situations we see around us. I know it may seem like I am going off on a rabbit trail here, but this all ties together. We will all encounter difficult, painful and heartbreaking situations in our lives. In fact, I believe that we need to go through these times before we can truly say that we are really maturing as a Christian.

It is when we go through these times and remain strong in our stand for our God that we can make the statement of faith that David made in Psalm 27: **"I would have lost hope if I did not believe that I see the goodness of the Lord, while in the land of the living." David was able to make this statement because he had been through the fire and survived! But he knew it was only through God's strength that he was able to do it.**

Faith and patience are two words that work closely together. Remember, it takes faith to wait patiently on the Lord, and it often takes waiting patiently before we really begin to see our faith work. Paul understood this. He says in Hebrews 6:11-12, **"And we desire that each one of you show the same diligence to the full assurance of hope until the end, that you do not become sluggish, but imitate those who through faith and patience inherit the promises."**

So, we see that it is through faith and patience that we inherit the promises. Abraham, Jacob, Moses, Joseph, David, Daniel and a multitude of others give us this example to follow.

Now let's go back to those verses in Psalm 27 and see what David is trying to tell us. As I said, there are three important things that we can get from these verses concerning faith and patience. Here are the verses again:

"¹³ *I would have lost heart,* **unless I had believed**
> **That I would see the goodness of the LORD**
> **In the land of the living.**

"¹⁴ **Wait on the LORD;**
> **Be of good courage,**
> **And He shall strengthen your heart;**
> **Wait, I say, on the LORD!"**

These verses really established themselves in my heart at a time in my life that I was uncertain about what I should be doing—not in terms of a career, but in my walk with the Lord. It was time for me to decide if I was "all in" when it came to God. I am sure many of you can relate to the position I was in. I was going to church regularly and had even begun to serve and tithe, but I knew God was asking for something more from me.

Was He, was Jesus Christ, going to be Lord over every part of my life? My struggle with this, just to be perfectly honest, was in knowing that I would be persecuted when I took that step. I knew there were friends that would walk away from me. So while it was not an intense fire that I was going through, it was still an intensity that was not easy for me to bear. So, as I sat on a merry-go-round in a park one day, reading the Bible, I came across these verses and they just seemed to jump out at me.

The first thing that God showed me was this: I needed to believe in His goodness. David **Believed!** He believed in God's goodness—and not just in the promise of going to Heaven one day, but that he would experience the goodness of the Lord here and now. This spoke to me. As I took this step of faith, I needed to completely submit every part of my life to God and trust Him completely—no matter what trials and 'fire' I had to endure. I could believe in His goodness! I really realized right then and there how important it was to *believe*. You have already read the part of this book on believing and know how much importance I put in it. Now you know where it started for me. Each of us, as Christians, must come to that place where we "believe and do not doubt."

The second thing that I learned from this verse is that even though I believe, there are going to be many times that I must **wait,** patiently. David learned and I have learned that while I am believing in what God is going to do, there are going to be many times that I will have to *wait* for what He is going to do. Waiting can be hard!

Tom Petty wrote a song where he says "the waiting is the hardest part." And it is! The word **wait** in in Psalm 27:14 is the Hebrew word **qavah** and means *to wait, to look for, to hope, and to expect*. David uses this word twice in this verse because he really understood the importance of *waiting on the Lord*. There are just going to be times in our lives when it seems like all is lost or, like in David's case, when it seems like everyone is against us. But it is during these times that we must take courage and wait, look for, hope and above all, expect God to come through for us. Again, it is during these times of trial and fire that we will be strengthened in our faith and in our will to persevere.

This leads me to the third important thing that I learned from this verse. In order to do the things that the word 'wait' means in Psalm 27:14, we must **be of good courage!** It is here you find that **He shall strengthen your heart.** To be patient and wait on our Father God when it seems like everything is falling down around us takes a lot of courage! To walk in faith takes courage! To believe you will see the goodness of the Lord *in the land of the living* takes courage! As I stated earlier in this book, the life of a true believer of Christ is not for the faint of heart. It is exciting and at times it is very challenging, but, above all, it is a life devoted to honoring God and receiving His promises!

Frank

Frank is a good friend of mine who is, at this moment of this writing, experiencing many of these challenges and rewards I am writing about. Almost 2 years ago, Frank was laid off from the position he held at a Chevrolet dealership as an auto body repairman. After about 2-3 months of being laid off, Frank came to me and said, "Pastor Mark, I think God is telling me to start my own business in auto body repair. But I just don't see how I can do it. I don't have any resources to invest in starting a business like that. What do you think I should do?"

I replied, "First of all, Frank, if you really think God is telling you to do this, then it really does not matter what I think! Secondly, I will commit to praying with you starting right now."

So we prayed together, asking God to make it clear to Frank what steps he should take. It soon became evident that this was definitely the direction that God wanted Frank to go. After much counsel with the right people and searching for the right place to begin doing business, Frank stepped out in faith and opened shop.

Right from the start, Frank did business the way the God would want him to. Even his business cards have the scripture, Proverbs 3:5-6, on the back of them. There were people that he felt God told him to bless with his work, and in obedience, Frank would do it. Time after time, God continued to bless Frank and open doors that needed to be opened. It did not mean that he didn't face opposition. There were many times Frank has come to me when the Devil was trying to throw a monkey wrench in God's plans. He would say with tears in his eyes, "Pastor Mark, I don't know what to do. I know this is what I am supposed to be doing, but it seems impossible right now!" I would pray with him and encourage him with Scripture. Sometimes, I reminded him to look at the Scripture on the back of his business card that reads:

"Trust in the Lord with all your heart and lean not on your own understanding; in all your ways acknowledge Him, and He will make your paths straight."

Frank would throw his shoulders back and say, "Yep, you are right. God knows what He is doing, and I have to trust in Him."

Just as often, he has come to me, again with tears in his eyes, sharing how God has supernaturally come through in those impossible situations.

Frank is learning the value and the benefit of waiting patiently on the Lord. He is also learning the importance of persevering through the trials we face in our lives. This principle of enduring through hardship is one of the most difficult to accept in our endeavor to become mature Christians. In the first book of

James, God tells us through the writer to "count it all joy when we fall into various trials." I used to laugh when I read this thinking, "Oh yeah, I am a bundle of joy when I am going through junk!" But the more I have matured as a Christian, the more I understand what God is trying to show us. James 1:2-4 says, **"My brethren, count it all joy when you fall into various trials, knowing that the testing of your faith produces patience. But let patience have *its* perfect work, that you may be perfect and complete, lacking nothing."**

The word 'patience' is used twice in this verse. It shows us that as our faith is tested, it produces patience. It is only when we allow patience to have its perfect work in us that we become truly perfected. But it is the 'allowing' that so many of us stumble on. Maybe Tom Petty's song should say, "the allowing is the hardest part!" Patience in this verse is the Greek word '**hypomone**' and means *steadfastness, constancy, endurance—the characteristic of a man who is not swerved from his deliberate purpose and his loyalty to faith and piety by even the greatest trials and suffering.*

In other words, to persevere! To remain strong and courageous and to not swerve in our loyalty to God and our faith! Be careful, however, this not a perseverance where we knuckle down, pull up our bootstraps and charge our way through whatever we are facing. It does not mean that we do not show any weakness. In fact, coming to a place of weakness and having no idea what to do is often right where God needs us to be. It is then that we will let go and allow Him to work in and through us. We simply need to persevere in our faith and in trusting that God will come through regardless of how bad things may look.

Now, this does not mean that you sit back and do nothing, waiting for God to wave some magic wand over you. True faith also involves work. The *trust* that we have in God most often involves believing that God will show us what to do, and then doing it. God gives us this example through His word in James 2:20-22:

"But do you want to know, O foolish man, that faith without works is dead? Was not Abraham our father justified by works when he offered Isaac his son on the altar? Do you see that faith was working together with his works, and by works faith was made perfect?"

In other words, Abraham trusted God so much that he was willing to do whatever God told him to do, trusting that God would stand by His promise to Abraham to make him 'the father of a multitude of nations.' It is often through our actions that our faith is made complete or 'perfect' as the Scripture above shows us. Again, this all involves patience and the willingness to wait on God and let Him show us what we are supposed to do.

So, if we think that being patient involves just sitting back and doing nothing while we wait to see what God is going to do, we will miss what God desires to show us in His Word. It takes a willingness to prepare and to work hard to walk in the will of God. He shows us this in Proverbs 21:5:

**"The plans of the diligent *lead* surely to plenty,
But *those of* everyone *who is* hasty, surely to poverty."**

The word 'diligent' here is the Greek word *'charuwts'* and means *sharp pointed decision, hard*. It is through good planning and hard work that we will find plenty in our lives, but hasty shortcuts will lead to poverty.

About 8 years ago, a friend of ours felt that God was telling him to go into the ministry full time, specifically to be part of a ministry based out of Texas. So, he made a decision to pack up his family, his wife and three children, and move to Texas. Several of his friends cautiously asked if he was sure of God's leading, that perhaps he should visit Texas on his own first to be sure that this was the direction that God was taking him. "No," he said, "we are going to trust that we are hearing God and just go."

Someone in the church was kind enough to give them a car and some money since they had nothing and off they went. To keep the story short, it was a disaster. When they got to Texas our friend did nothing, believing that God was going to open the door to get into the ministry they thought they were supposed to be a part of. It didn't take very long until they were out of money and literally living on the streets and sleeping in their car.

He finally looked for work and was able to get a job and keep his family off the streets. Even then, he went from job to job and continued struggling financially until finally he brought his family back to Michigan. Sadly, he blamed God for how things worked out. He walked away from his faith and his family and still refuses to take advice from godly men around him.

Now I know there are times that God will ask us to step out in faith but—and this is directed mostly toward you men out there—I do not believe that God would ever ask us to put our wives and children in jeopardy to follow His will!

I have another good friend who believed that God was calling him to leave the comfort of his job with Spring Hill Camps and to venture out on his own in ministry, working with the World Orphans organization. He began to work hard and prepare, laying the ground work as God showed him before he took that first step out on his own. It still took faith and has continued to take faith since they count on the outside support of other people to take care of their needs, but he works hard, trusts God, and prays hard in each step that God shows him to take. Because of his *diligence* he is thriving in that ministry after almost 2 years of working it. He is impacting orphans and churches all around the word, and his family is doing wonderfully. Ultimately, it has been through his faith *and* his patience that he has had success in his endeavors.

Faith and Patience are Partners

Hopefully you are beginning to see that faith and patience work hand in hand together. They are a team that function together to help us when we chose to believe in God's promises. God shows us this through His word in Hebrews 6:11-12:

"And we desire that each one of you show the same diligence to the full assurance of hope until the end, that you do not become sluggish, but imitate those who through faith and patience inherit the promises."

We need to imitate those who, through faith and patience, inherit the promises. We are given great testimonies in the Old and New Testament of people who, through their faith in the promises of God, persevered and endured through the most trying and difficult of circumstances. The word 'patience' in this verse is the Greek word '**makrothymia**' and means *patience, forbearance, and slowness in avenging wrongs.* Interestingly, this is the same word used over and over throughout the Bible to portray God's **longsuffering** towards His people. He is patient and forbearing and slow in avenging wrongs. In other words, no matter how often we mess up, He is there waiting for us to throw up our arms in surrender and admit that we need Him. God is patiently waiting for us to humble ourselves and give the situation to Him. Like any good father, God, in His longsuffering, waits on His sons and daughters to turn to Him in complete submission. In 2 Peter 3:9, it is stated this way:

"The Lord is not slack concerning *His* promise, as some count slackness, but is longsuffering toward us, not willing that any should perish but that all should come to repentance."

What a beautiful example of a Father who will never give up on His sons or daughters. No matter how often we turn our faces away from Him or slap Him in the face with our pride and insolence, God is lovingly waiting for us.

The easiest way for me to understand this is to look at how I feel about my own sons. I have two amazing sons but, like any of us, they are not without faults. Through any of the difficult situations we have experienced with them, Stephanie and I have always gone back to the promises God gives us in His Word. Add to that the vision He has given us for them and we do not waver from what He has shown us. Regardless of any ugliness they may extend towards, us we are longsuffering in our actions toward them. We never give up on them!

God is the same way towards us! No matter what we do He is there, waiting with arms open, never giving up on us. He gives us an amazing example of how we must conduct our lives towards all people, not just our sons and daughters. We see God's heart has towards all people in the second part of the passage in 2 Peter 3:9 where it says that the Lord is not willing that **any** should perish but that **all** should come to repentance. We have to remember something when we read this verse. See, we are created in God's image (Genesis 1:26), and we are renewed in the knowledge of Him who created us (Colossians 3:10). Since this is true, then we are to exhibit the same *longsuffering* towards the people around us that God shows towards each and every person on this earth. This is tied directly to what I showed you about love earlier in this book. Remember what it says in Luke 6:27-28:

"But I say to you who hear: Love your enemies, do good to those who hate you, bless those who curse you, and pray for those who spitefully use you."

Of course we can only do this with God's help. When we try to do it on our own, the burden can become so crushing that is can literally affect our health in a negative way. To be longsuffering in the way that God's Word wants us to be—being patient, forbearing and slow in avenging wrongs—can only be done in God's strength, not our own.

In the past two years, God has brought me through an experience that has taught me more about this facet of patience than at any other time in my life. My Heavenly Father has taught me the importance of longsuffering, and I also learned, first hand, about the negative side effects of trying to do it on my own. Let me share the story with you.

A little over two years ago, God began to reveal things to me about the way things were being done within the church that I am on staff as a pastor at. The alarming thing was that these things involved the senior staff, from our lead pastor down—including myself. Our church was growing at a very rapid rate. In a few short years, we had grown from a church of

300 or so to a church of almost 2,000. And this was in a town of only about 10,000.

Things seemed to be going great. Momentum was in high gear and it appeared that God was really blessing us. In fact, I really believe He was. There were a lot of great things happening. People were giving their lives to Christ and lives were really changing for the better. Indeed, I was learning so much being on staff under this lead pastor about God's Word, how to lead and execute properly, and how to operate efficiently and effectively. While all these things were great, we began to have a sense that there was something that was just not right. It became apparent to us that our focus had taken a turn off of where it needed to be. In fact, what happened was the same thing that happens to most successful churches or businesses. The success began to point more towards man than to God.

God warns us about this so often in His Word, and yet all through history, we just seem to keep stumbling into this pit called PRIDE. God warns us about it in Deuteronomy 8:18-19:

"And you shall remember the LORD your God, for *it is* He who gives you power to get wealth, that He may establish His covenant which He swore to your fathers, as *it is* this day. Then it shall be, if you by any means forget the LORD your God, and follow other gods, and serve them and worship them, I testify against you this day that you shall surely perish."

The gods that we had begun to follow as a church were pride, self-sufficiency, and a man.

Now, here is where the longsuffering part came in for Stephanie and I. The first thing I really began to notice was a deterioration of my lead pastor's family relationships. In fact, I began to see problems with all the marriages of the pastors on staff. A mix-up of God's priorities began to occur. The work of the ministry began to take on more importance than the emotional, physical and spiritual well being of our families. This happened even in my own family.

I began to notice it first in my oldest son. He was really acting out with a lot of anger. Then Stephanie began to voice to me that the ministry seemed to be more important than our family. That stopped me cold as I remembered something that the Lord had spoke to me years before. This is what he told me then and reminded me of at that time.: "Mark, if you can't minister in your own home then I will never really be able to use you to effectively minister outside of your home." This is really a directive to us in God's Word found in 1 Timothy 3:4-5:

"...one who rules his own house well, having *his* children in submission with all reverence (for if a man does not know how to rule his own house, how will he take care of the church of God?)"

In this verse, God is talking to the overseers of His church and, as pastors, that meant us!

I began to pray about what I should do and was lead to sit down with our lead pastor and express my concerns. I was careful in how I went about it, not wanting to show a lack of respect for the position of authority he held. I spoke of my concerns that the marriages and families on staff were suffering due to the preeminence that we had put the ministry and church in. He did not receive it. He did not exactly rebuke me, but he did make it clear that he did not believe I knew what I was talking about.

Nevertheless, Stephanie and I began to prayerfully consider everything we did with the church and the ministry. We began to put more emphasis on our marriage and family. There were things that we respectfully declined to be a part of if it began to affect our ability to have time together as a family. Due to the stance we took, we were essentially 'blacklisted' so to speak. It seemed as if they were saying, "Let's give Pastor Mark a little corner and just leave him alone there." We later learned that this is actually what was said in one of the staff leadership meetings that were held without us. We also heard comments like "Mark and Stephanie have drawn a line in the sand and are not sold out to the ministry." While we felt hurt by these comments, we also agreed to a certain extent with what they were saying. We weren't sold out to the *ministry;* we were only sold out to *God!* I refused to sacrifice my family on the altar of the ministry!

Stephanie and I really began to focus on our relationship with Father God and with each other. As those two areas remained strong, God used us in the ministry that He continued to ask us to be a part of. While we were doing this, we watched as the pride and deception grew worse in the church. Finally, almost two years after I spoke to our lead pastor about my concerns, it came out that he was having an affair with our worship leader. This came as no surprise to me as I had confronted him 3 months earlier concerning his relationship with her.

Of course they were both asked to step down from their positions in the church. As the church rallied to stay together after this devastating blow, it soon became apparent that the pride and deception still had not left the church despite the blow we had taken. What followed can only be explained as a political race for the lead pastor position that was bred out of an attitude of entitlement.

For the next several months, the church seemed to be holding together amazingly well, but the condition of the remaining staff became worse and worse as camps began to form around individuals. During this time, Stephanie and I believe the Lord put us in the position of **watchmen.** We got this through several Scriptures and through words that were spoken to us. We were told by one of these people to read in Ezekiel chapters 3 and 33. Ezekiel 3:16-17 says this:

"Now it came to pass at the end of seven days that the word of the LORD came to me, saying, 'Son of man, I have made you a watchman for the house of Israel; therefore hear a word from My mouth, and give them warning from Me.'"

This was the position that Stephanie and I felt the Lord was asking us to be in. There were occasions when He told us to speak and times when He told us to hold our tongue. The times that He told us to speak were towards those who were in authority and vying for the position of lead pastor. These individuals had many supporters and the words we brought them were not words they wanted to hear, and each time we did what God asked us to do, we received heavy fire. But it accomplished what God desired and the right person was brought into the position of lead pastor.

It was not easy, but we knew we were doing what God was asking us to. We were longsuffering. But when we understand how longsuffering God is towards us, out of His tremendous love for us, then we are able to be longsuffering for His sake.

As we go through difficult times of tribulation and persecution, it is by remembering how much God loves us and that He will always deliver us that we can trust in, believe in, and wait on Him. Paul gives us an example of this time and time again throughout the New Testament. In 2 Timothy 3:10-11, he speaks of it this way:

"But you have carefully followed my doctrine, manner of life, purpose, faith, longsuffering, love, perseverance, persecutions, afflictions, which happened to me at Antioch, at Iconium, at Lystra—what persecutions I endured. And out of *them* all the Lord delivered me."

Paul speaks of longsuffering, perseverance, persecutions and afflictions, but he makes this statement at the end: "And out of them all the Lord delivered me." God will deliver us from all of these kinds of circumstances but first we must be willing to be obedient to, trust in, and believe in Him! Through faith and patience we can accomplish this.

The Benefits of Waiting Patiently

There are many benefits to waiting patiently on the Lord, more than what I am going to talk about here, but these are six specific benefits I have identified clearly in my life that I want to share with you. None of them are easy, but I want to encourage you that if you will seek them, identify them, and walk in them, then it is worth the effort!

Character Development

Psalm 25:21 – Let integrity and uprightness preserve me, for I wait for You.

David, the king of Israel, was a man of character. He was not a perfect man who never made mistakes, but he *was* a man who loved the Lord and desired to get right with God when he did mess up. That takes character. The word **'wait'** in this verse is the same Hebrew word that is used in Psalm 27 that we looked at earlier. It means to wait, to look for, to hope or to expect.

What we fail to realize is that character building often takes place in the trials and tribulations in our lives. Paul shows us this in Romans 5:3-4 where he says, **"And not only *that*, but we**

also glory in tribulations, knowing that tribulation produces perseverance; and perseverance, character; and character, hope."

Notice that character comes *after* tribulation and perseverance. It is at the end of it all that we find hope in a God that loves us more than we can comprehend.

It is character that will sustain or preserve us. We can be the most gifted communicator, leader, financial mind, or technological wizard, but it is only our character that will sustain us. We will reach a certain level of success, but without integrity and uprightness, we will eventually fall.

Strengthening Our Heart

Psalm 27:14 – Wait on the LORD; Be of good courage And He shall strengthen your heart; Wait, I say, on the LORD!

Our heart is so important to God. In fact, it is so important to Him that He speaks of the heart 926 times throughout the Old and New Testament! All through the Bible there are accounts of men and women who endured through trying circumstances and waited on God with hopeful expectation for Him to come through with the promises He had made them. Abraham was one of these men. In Hebrews 6:15, we read, **"And so, after he had patiently endured, he obtained the promise."**

See, when Abraham was about 70 years old, God spoke to him and told him he would have a son (Genesis 15). At the same time, God told Abraham that he would have descendants that would number the stars in the sky! Abraham had to have been ecstatic. In fact, he probably went and told some of his friends what God had told him. But then 10 years past and nothing happened. His friends probably made fun of him and eventually dismissed what he had said.

I am sure many of you have been in this same situation. God speaks something to you and when you tell friends or family, they simply laugh or dismiss what you say, especially if it does not happen immediately. But, just like Abraham, we must wait and allow God to strengthen our heart. 20 years later, Abraham was still waiting. Now, by this time, he might have been thinking, "Okay, maybe I just dreamed what I thought God told me." But I don't think so. I believe he held on and endured. Finally, after more than 30 years, Abraham sees the promise fulfilled. The word 'patiently' in the verse above is the Greek word 'Makrothymeo' and means to be of a long spirit and to not lose *heart*. Abraham did not lose heart and he received the promise. When we wait on God, the same thing will happen for us.

Learning to Endure

Hebrews 10:35-36 – Therefore do not cast away your confidence, which has great reward. For you have need of endurance, so that after you have done the will of God, you may receive the promise...

We have need of endurance! In fact, I believe that we live in a time that requires Christians to endure more than ever.

I hear people, Christians, all around me talking about how bad things are getting. They mutter about how horrible the economy is, about all the sickness, about the terrible tragedies happening around the world. They allow it to bring fear into their hearts. We must remember that these times are expected! Jesus speaks of these things in Matthew chapter 24:6-8:

"And you will hear of wars and rumors of wars. See that you are not troubled; for all *these things* must come to pass, but the end is not yet. For nation will rise against nation, and kingdom against kingdom. And there will be famines, pestilences, and earthquakes in various places. All these *are* the beginning of sorrows."

See that you are not troubled. As Christians we must not let fear come in. Instead, we must realize that these are things that *must come to pass.* In other words, when you know that God is still in control, it will be your strength of heart and endurance that will encourage other people.

But, Jesus also says to us in Matthew 6:25, "Do not worry!" Then He goes on to say in Matthew 6 verse 33 to seek God first in everything and we will be taken care of! So, we must learn to endure so we "may receive the promise."

The word 'endurance' in Hebrews 10:36 is actually the word *'patience'* in the King James Bible. It is the Greek word **'hypomone'** and means *steadfastness, constancy and endurance.* So as we endure through these difficult times that we are in, we must be steadfast, constant and enduring. And really, if we think about it, we *must* be that kind of person—or Christian—

for all those people out there who do not have that "anchor for the soul" (Hebrews 6:19) that we have in Jesus Christ.

"So after we have done the will of God…" Sometimes, I believe that "doing the will of God" is simply enduring and waiting on Him. And as we do this, the Bible tells us that we will be blessed. Read with me in James 1 verse 12:

"Blessed *is* the man who endures temptation; for when he has been approved, he will receive the crown of life which the Lord has promised to those who love Him."

I believe this! I have seen it happen over and over in my own life and in the lives of others who *believe* God's Word without compromise. The hard part in this for most of us, me included, is that we don't want to go through the enduring to get the blessing. But we will go through testing and temptation! That word '**temptation**' in James 1:12 is the Greek word '**parasmo's**' and has a great translation. It means *the trial of a man's fidelity, integrity, virtue and constancy.* It comes back to character again. Where are we going to stand when the heat gets turned up? If we believe in the Word of God, we will "trust in the Lord our God" and stand on His Word!

Circumcision of the Heart

Deuteronomy 30:6 – And the LORD your God will circumcise your heart and the heart of your descendants, to love the LORD your God with all your heart and with all your soul, that you may live.

As the Master Physician, God desires to make our heart whole and healthy, but He can only do this if we will allow Him to. He knows that our hearts are sick, but so often we don't see it or realize it. We know it is there, but in our self-righteousness, won't acknowledge it. Our hearts *are* sick, however, and no matter how mature we become as Christians, there is always more that God wants to clean out of us. In the book of Jeremiah, God shows us the condition of our heart when He says in Jeremiah 17:9:

"The heart *is* deceitful above all *things*,
And desperately wicked;
Who can know it?"

We cannot know our own heart unless we allow God to show us the things that are hidden in it. There is always more that needs to be cleaned out of us, or circumcised and 'surgically' removed. We are in great danger when we get to a place that we feel that our own heart is pure and without fault. While it is God's purpose and desire to make our hearts pure, to become more like the one who created us (Colossians 3:10), our flesh, the world, and the Devil will constantly be fighting to keep us from reaching that point. The beauty of God's plan is that a willing and repentant heart will keep us close to Him and allow Him to test us! Read verse ten of that same chapter in Jeremiah and allow it to humbly show you what I am trying to say here.

"I, the LORD, search the heart,
I test the mind,
Even to give every man according to his ways,
According to the fruit of his doings."

We can say or think all we want, but it is the fruit of what we *do* that will show if we are really willing to allow God to circumcise our hearts.

We are shown this same principle in the New Testament where Jesus is addressing the issue in Matthew 12:33-35:

"Either make the tree good and its fruit good, or else make the tree bad and its fruit bad; for a tree is known by *its* fruit. Brood of vipers! How can you, being evil, speak good things? For out of the abundance of the heart the mouth speaks. A good man out of the good treasure of his heart brings forth good things, and an evil man out of the evil treasure brings forth evil things."

Again, we are shown that it comes back to the heart and the fruit that comes from what is in it. Our lives will be an exhibit of what is really in our hearts, especially when we go through testing or fire. It is really similar to the process of purifying silver. For silver to be purified, it is placed in a pot with intense heat underneath it. As the silver comes to a boil, all the junk or dross within comes to the surface so that it can be removed. This process is done over and over until the silver becomes as pure as possible. God does the same thing with our hearts. The heat is turned up and what is really within will come to the surface. It is easy to say that we live for God in righteousness when everything is rosy, but it is when our lives are squeezed and the pressure is turned on that we see what is really in our hearts.

A little earlier, I shared with you the struggles that Stephanie and I went through as we served on staff in our church. As we neared the end of this battle, we were amazed that we had been able to keep an attitude of joy and peace in the mist of that trial. We knew that God had sustained us since we were obedient to the things that He asked us to do.

Strangely, enough, it was at the end of the battle that things went wrong for us. And I realize now, looking back, that it was due to what I had allowed to come into my heart all through that time of testing. It took one final attack against me and my integrity to bring to the surface what was really hidden in my heart. What came out was offense. We allowed the joy and peace that we had been experiencing to be replaced by thoughts of anger towards the people involved and towards God for allowing it to happen.

Suddenly we felt lost, bitter, and uncertain. The presence of God that I had always felt had disappeared. But this is exactly what happens when we allow the wrong things, or sin, into our hearts. When sin is present and we don't see it, then we are distanced from God.

Amazingly, it took almost three months to realize what we had allowed in. Through circumstances, God's Word, and people who I allowed to speak into my life, I was given the revelation of where my heart was. I literally fell to the floor weeping when I realized where I had allowed my relationship with God to go. It was a beautiful time of repentance and reconnecting with my amazing Heavenly Father! After this, God showed us the steps we needed to take to completely remove the offense and bitterness from our hearts. It was not easy, but we were obedient to what He showed us, and the freedom that came afterwards was wonderful.

The process of waiting on God and letting Him circumcise those areas of our hearts that need it is never easy, but it is only through the removal of these impurities that He can get us to where He wants us to be. And where is that place? It is in a relationship with our Heavenly Father where "we love Him with all our heart and with all of our soul, that we may live!"

Faith That Endures

Psalm 40:1-2 – [1] I waited patiently for the LORD;
        And He inclined to me,
        And heard my cry.
[2] He also brought me up out of a horrible pit,
        Out of the miry clay,
        And set my feet upon a rock,
        And **established my steps.**

King David had such an amazing relationship with God! He was not perfect. In fact, he messed up a lot. But he gives us such a wonderful example of his willingness to repent when he did mess up and how to keep trusting and waiting on God in all situations.

If we look at verse one above, we see that David writes about patiently waiting for the Lord. If we look at the Hebrew translation of the words, we will find that it is not the kind of waiting many people think of when "waiting on the Lord." In fact, both of the words 'waited' and 'patiently' are the *same* Hebrew word when translated. They are the Hebrew word **'Qavah'** that we looked at earlier in Psalm 27. And if you remember, this word means *to wait, to look for, to hope or to expect.*

So when we look at the word 'wait' that David uses here, it is not the 'sitting around and waiting, complacent or depressed, wondering when God is going to do' kind of waiting. No, as David waited, he waited with *hope, a looking forward to, while expecting* God to do something for him. He truly believed—or had faith—that God was going to do what was stated in verse two of Psalm 40. That he would be brought up out of a horrible pit, out of the miry clay, that his feet would be placed upon a rock, and his steps established. David believed so strongly in this kind of waiting that he used the same word twice to emphasize both 'waiting' and 'patiently.'

It is when we are willing to wait in this fashion that our faith will become strong enough to trust that, in every circumstance, God is going to work things out for His glory. As I stated earlier in this section of the book, it takes faith to be patient and wait on the Lord, *and* so often, it is when we wait patiently that our faith is strengthened and allowed to work. But we must have faith and wait upon the Lord, believing that He is going to come through with the promises that He gives us in His Word.

Concluding Thoughts

When I began this book, I asked the question, "What is faith?" It is not something we can touch, but it is something we can live by. The New Testament gives us two primary translations for the word 'faith' in the context that it is used. One is the Greek word *'pistis'* and means a *conviction of the truth of anything, belief; in the NT of a conviction or belief respecting man's relationship to God and divine things.* Essentially, it is a conviction in the truth of who God is and what His Word says. Jesus uses this word in Matthew 9:22:

"But Jesus turned around, and when He saw her He said, 'Be of good cheer, daughter; your faith has made you well.' And the woman was made well from that hour."

When this poor woman, who had been sick for 12 years, simply had faith that if she touched the hem of Jesus' garment she would be made whole, it was done for her! Look what Jesus said, "Your faith has make you well." This was faith that believed in a God that desired to see her whole. Even more, God wants these supernatural occurrences to cause us to desire more of His presence!

The second way that the word 'faith' is portrayed in the New Testament is through the Greek word *'olegopestos.'* It means *of little faith or trusting too little*. We are given an example of this word when Jesus speaks to His disciples in Matthew 16:8:

"But Jesus, being aware of *it*, said to them, 'O you of little faith, why do you reason among yourselves because you have brought no bread?'"

We are shown here that we can have a *negative* faith that does not work positively for us. In other words, we can possess a faith that does *not* believe what we need or desire will happen. True faith is belief in what we need or desire even before we see it. Hebrews 11:1 gives us a great definition of this where it says, **"Now faith is the substance of things hoped for, the evidence of things not seen."**

The word 'substance' in that verse is the Greek word *'hypostasis'* and means *that which has foundation, is firm and that which has actual existence*. So, again, God is showing us in His Word that true faith is believing that something exists even before we see it.

Stephanie and I continue to walk in faith as we move along on this journey that God has us on. Our church continues to struggle and we still have questions about what the future holds. Despite this we continue to trust in God, knowing that He is in control. We have to constantly remind ourselves that the church is His and that our faith is not dependant on whether the doors remain open or not. What is most important is that we keep our faith and relationship strong with Father God.

I hope and I pray that as you read through this book something sparked inside of you. That as you have seen how Love, God's Word, Speaking and Believing, and Patience are pivotal in growing and sustaining our faith, that you were inspired, ultimately to live a life fully devoted to our God and Savior. To really truly live a life of faith is to be a person that is running hard after the presence of God and never, ever getting enough of Him!